ADHD Solution Deck: Cleaning

The Fast, Simple, Efficient Cleaning System

Lily Beacham

Contents

For my Mum,
"The Queen of Clean"

To the Reader

I have written this book with you, the reader in mind, and I don't just mean the tips, strategies, and systems I discuss. I wanted to make this book as easy a read as possible for people who are neurodivergent, so the words in this book are printed in a special accessibility font.

Short paragraphs, sub-headings, bullet points, and chapter summaries have been used so that the information is easy to follow and refer back to. I hope that this makes your reading experience better.

Lily Beacham

Introduction

You step into your best friend's home for a relaxing cup of coffee. You go with them to the kitchen to help prepare it, but find yourself almost zoned out of the conversation as you admire their shiningly clean kitchen counters. Once the coffee is ready, you go to the lounge. You are so used to dodging toys at your house that you simply can't get your children to pick up that your eyes automatically fix to the floor. Instead of seeing toys scattered all over the floor, all you see are immaculately clean tiles, without even a cookie crumb lying somewhere in a corner.

As you sit on the couch, you again find your mind drifting even more, while your senses are working overtime. You take in the scents, but all you get is a slight linger of cleaning products that must've been used that morning. Your hand touches the side table to pick up your coffee mug, and there is not a speckle of dust. You look around you and see even the windows are sparkling clean.

Introduction

Suddenly, your "relaxing" coffee is anything but a time to decompress and unwind. Instead, you find your throat closing up as a rush of stress, anxiety, and even a lack of self-worth comes over you. *Why can't my house be this clean? Why must I always have to make excuses for the state of my house when someone stops by unannounced? Why can't I have it all together? Why am I so overwhelmed by my dirty house that I don't know where to start? Why must I have ADHD?* These questions mull through your brain for the rest of this coffee date.

On your way home, you decide this is now the time things will change. *My place will no longer look like a pigsty. I don't have to live like this. I can have a home that I can be proud of.* As you get home, you immediately grab the broom, mop, and vacuum and go through your house like a hurricane. Along the way, you scold your children for leaving their toys all over the place.

Once the house is clean, you call the whole family together to lay down the new law. "We will keep this clean. We will not live like this anymore," you tell them. *This is going to be great,* you think. However, a week later, you find yourself in the same mess. Toys lying all over the floor, crumbs covering your counters, and a bathroom that looks like it hasn't been cleaned in a year. Your self-esteem takes yet another dive. *I can't even keep my home clean for longer than a week. I'm a failure,* you cry.

If this sounds similar to your life, you don't have to lose all hope. Even though cleaning can be more difficult if you have a condition like ADHD, it is not impossible. If you make changes to the way you view and go about cleaning, you can have that clean home you desire. You have come to the right place.

While the examples in this book might not match your exact situation at home, I want to stress that this cleaning system is most definitely for anyone and everyone. **The Fast, Simple, Efficient Cleaning System** will help you all. It is very easy to adapt to your circumstances and home.

This book will provide you with helpful guides and tips on how to make cleaning **Fast, Simple, and Efficient**. I will help you realize that cleaning is not just a project, but rather an ongoing practice. Your home will never stay clean. That is part of life. I will help you to change your mindset about having a perfect home. You don't have to live in a *show home*. It's too hard to maintain. Instead, you just need to get it done and enjoy your five-second win when it is all clean and neat. Create your own new version of perfect.

I understand the challenges that people with ADHD face on a daily basis. I will discuss the potential problems that people with ADIID can experience which can make cleaning difficult. These include:

- time blindness
- distractibility
- impulsivity
- disorganization
- procrastination

Due to these factors, people with ADHD are often overwhelmed by cleaning tasks, no matter how much they want to have a clean home. One of my daughters (a millennial in her 20s) has ADHD and gets completely overwhelmed by organizational tasks such as cleaning. Due to her hyperfocus, she also easily loses track of time. All of this has led her to feel inadequate and stressed, and to have low self-esteem.

Throughout her life, I have seen how she struggles to complete cleaning tasks. She now lives with her partner and both of them have very demanding jobs; as a result, she has almost no time to clean her home.

With a background in interior design and home organization, I have created a system that makes cleaning easy and achievable for even the most unorganized person. This system has helped my daughter and countless other people with ADHD to achieve the clean home they desire. Now I want to help you. I love this system so much that I use it in my own home. It is flexible enough to adapt to any home situation and the principles are easy to implement and follow.

Through *ADHD Solution Deck: Cleaning* I will arm you with the knowledge, tools, and processes that can make cleaning **Fast, Simple and Efficient**, and transform your life. My tried and tested solutions to cleaning difficulties include:

- Get it done. It doesn't have to be perfect.
- You don't have to deep clean every time you clean.
- Create your own cleaning goals.
- Do a quick cyclone clean.
- Complete your daily five cleaning tasks.
- Implement zone cleaning.
- Create cleaning schedules according to your zones.
- Use the right techniques to clean efficiently.

You will also be given free access to my exclusive resource file, which includes the following:

- cleaning schedule templates
- an example of a weekly zone cleaning schedule
- monthly, seasonal, bi-annual, and annual cleaning checklists
- a tracker for cleaning tasks ("When did I last...")
- more than 20 homemade cleaning recipes
- a list of pet-friendly essential oils

These schedules will help you to put your plan into action and you can work toward having a cleaner space and a clearer mind. So, let's get straight into it and discuss how you can get over the obstacles your ADHD can create.

Chapter 1
Why Is Cleaning So Difficult?

Cleaning a house can seem like a never-ending chore. You might have just finished doing the dishes or unpacking the dishwasher. However, you will need to eat again, resulting in more dirty dishes. You could have just finished washing, drying, and packing away your laundry. Unfortunately, unless you decide to live naked for the rest of your life, your laundry basket will fill again soon. Maybe you have just finished cleaning your house. You opened the windows to get fresh air into the house. Suddenly, the wind picks up, blowing leaves and other dirt into your clean house.

Like I've said, cleaning your house can feel like you are never truly winning. This is particularly the case if you have young children. These tiny humans tend to leave their toys all over the house, you might find dirty socks in the oddest of places, and the minute you finish washing the floors, they will mess their sticky juice all over them.

Unless you have a passion for cleaning, this task can seem so impossibly huge that you simply don't even know where to start. It may seem even more overwhelming for those who have been diagnosed with attention deficit hyperactivity disorder (ADHD).

The Impact of ADHD

Having ADHD means you will feel like you have a lot more on your plate, and you might struggle to get started on your task. This doesn't mean you are lazy at all. The fact that you're struggling to get tasks like cleaning done, is rather due to factors such as:

- having difficulty staying on task or paying attention.
- daydreaming or tuning out.
- having hyperfocus that can cause you to lose track of time.
- being impulsive.
- struggling with organizational issues.

All of this can make cleaning feel like it can be an impossible task, especially since it is not a task you can do and put to bed, but have to do constantly to stay on top of. Let's look at various ways ADHD can cause you to struggle to either get started or complete your cleaning tasks.

Time Blindness

Many people with ADHD have hyperfocus. This can cause you to focus so intently on what you are doing that you tune out everything else going on in your life. As much as this can be a fantastic attribute to have in completing certain tasks, it can cause you to lose track of time, often referred to as time blindness. It might feel like you have only been busy with something for five minutes when it has actually been more than two hours.

This can cause you to miss deadlines, be late for events (even if you are excited about them), and not get started on tasks that do not interest you. Unless you have a passion for cleaning, time blindness can cause you to never have enough time to clean your home.

There are ways of working around this. You can make your hyperfocus work for you without it going into time blindness:

- Make sure you have everything you need for the cleaning job before you start. Every time you need to go fetch something you have forgotten, you run the risk of getting distracted. Have checklists for every task, so you know what you need before you start.
- Determine what you need to create the right mood for you to clean. Do you enjoy blasting the radio and dancing while cleaning? Do you prefer listening to a podcast? Do you need dead quiet around you to be able to focus?
- Eliminate all distractions. This can mean switching off the television, closing your laptop, or putting your phone on silent.
- Decide how long you will work before you allow yourself a break. This will depend on your individual needs and limitations. Some people can work for 30 minutes straight without taking a break, others shorter, or longer. Decide what works for you.

- After you have decided how much time you will spend cleaning, set a timer. When the alarm rings and you feel like you can continue with your specific task, snooze it if you like. However, make sure you are still busy with the specific task, and that you have not (without realizing it) gone over to another task.
- When you take a break, drink a glass of water. A person's brain works best when it is hydrated, so make sure you consume enough fluids when you need to concentrate. Stick to your time limits for this break. If you allow yourself a ten-minute break, set a timer and go back to your task as soon as it rings.
- Once your break is over, rinse and repeat. Do this over and over until your task has been completed.

Distractibility

One of the main symptoms of ADHD is being easily distracted. Even the slightest distraction (someone writing with a pen next to you at work or a dog barking a couple of streets away) can cause you to lose focus. This can result in difficulty completing tasks, and ultimately, make you feel incompetent.

It is important to remind yourself that being easily distracted doesn't make you incompetent. It just means you will need to find techniques to make coping with these distractions easier for you.

- Set daily cleaning goals; for example, today I am going to clean the living room. You now know exactly what you need to do. Once you start, break the big task of cleaning the space up into smaller tasks, such as sorting, dusting, vacuuming, etc. Focus on one small task at a time. Finish that task first before moving to the next.

- Another way to reduce your distractibility is by doing the task you dislike most first. You are more likely to get distracted doing something you don't enjoy. Get that done first.
- If you feel negative about a task before you even start, you will increase the chances of getting distracted. If you can manage your emotions by being aware of when you have negative feelings toward a task and changing that to trying to be positive, you will most likely find yourself completing tasks easier.
- Be conscious of your mind and your thoughts. If you find your mind drifting from the task at hand, bring it back. For example, if you are washing the dishes, make a conscious effort to only think about washing the dishes.
- Another way to improve your focus is by giving yourself less time to complete a task. If you know something will take, on average, 20 minutes to complete, set a timer for 15 minutes and try to complete it before the timer goes off. This will force you to focus and get it done.

Impulsivity

Being impulsive is another symptom that many people with ADHD suffer from daily. This can cause you to stop the cleaning tasks you are busy with halfway through to act on your impulsive urges. This results firstly in you not completing your tasks, secondly in you becoming frustrated with yourself and the situation, and lastly in feeling overwhelmed as the tasks just keep increasing.

- To try and avoid this from happening, be mindful of when you want to give in to your impulsive urges. Once you become aware that you are about to stop your task before completing it, do whatever you need to do to keep at it.
- This can mean pep-talking yourself back to your task, setting yourself some sort of "punishment" if you don't complete the task first, or rewarding yourself for doing it.
- Stick to doing one task at a time. If you try to multitask, you are more likely to lose focus and give in to urges.
- It can also help to put on calming music to keep your mind from drifting to your impulsive urges, or do deep breathing practices to keep you focused on the task at hand.

Disorganization

Being (and feeling) unorganized is another problem that many people with ADHD have to deal with on a daily basis. This is often rooted out of a fear that what you need to organize won't be perfect. It can also be that you overcommit yourself, resulting in even more disorganization in your life.

When it comes to cleaning your house, don't overcommit to wanting to organize your entire home in a single day. This is unrealistic and is bound to leave you feeling anxious about the mess that organizing can create—you might find yourself sitting on the floor with all the contents from all your cupboards scattered all around you. You may have started out with the clear intention of organizing it all, but now, the task is overwhelming.

- Avoid this by breaking your cleaning tasks into small, achievable tasks. If you want to organize your home, do it one rack in a cupboard at a time. If you want to clean, do it one room at a time. The feeling of completing these tasks will help you to realize that you can do it, which can motivate you to take on another task.
- Use your "wasted" minutes to complete a task. The average electric kettle takes between two to four minutes to boil. While you are waiting for this, unpack the dishwasher, do the dishes, or clean a shelf in the kitchen. Once you have created a habit of doing this, your tasks around the kitchen will decrease almost automatically, leaving you feeling accomplished and freeing up more time for other tasks.
- Struggling to make decisions can also cause you to feel disorganized. This can be avoided by having an organized cleaning system in place. By doing this, you will avoid having to worry about deciding what to clean each day.

Procrastination

All these factors mentioned above contribute to a bigger problem you might experience: procrastination. People who procrastinate often make excuses for this, or find reasons why they need to put off starting their tasks.

- *"I don't like cleaning"*: Remind yourself that not many people actually enjoy cleaning, but most people want to live in a clean home. Look for ways to make cleaning more fun. For example, listen to music or a podcast while you clean.
- *"I am overwhelmed by the amount of cleaning I need to do"*: Break the task up into smaller tasks. For example, break your task of doing laundry up into different steps:
- take all the dirty clothes to the laundry
- sort your laundry
- put the first load in the washer
- add the second load as soon as the first load is done
- fold and pack away as soon as the clothes are dry
- create a laundry schedule so you don't have to do all your laundry in one day.
- *"I struggle to start a cleaning task"*: I have mentioned this before, but start with the task you dislike the most first. This task is likely hanging over you like a dark cloud. Once you get that task done, you may feel ready to take on the next.
- *"I find cleaning too difficult"*: If you have all the tools (cleaning products and equipment) you will need, no cleaning task will be difficult after following the helpful tips in this book. I will even help you with checklists of everything you need to clean the different spaces in your house.

Chapter Summary

There are many factors that can make cleaning with ADHD difficult, as you might not know where to start or what to do. However, if you follow the steps to keep your focus on the things that matter and the task at hand, you can have the clean home you have always dreamed of.

Time Blindness

- Have everything you will need ready before you start.
- Set the right mood to clean and eliminate all distractions.
- Decide on a timeframe, set an alarm, and remember to drink some water when you take a break.

Distractibility

- Set daily cleaning goals for yourself so you know exactly what needs to be done.
- Do the task you dislike first, and then the rest of your tasks will be easier and more pleasant.
- Manage your emotions and thoughts while you are cleaning.
- Give yourself slightly less time than you actually need to complete the task.

Impulsivity

- Always be mindful of your impulsive urges.
- Give yourself a pep talk if you feel yourself giving in to your urges.

- Stick to one task at a time.

Disorganization

- Break your cleaning jobs into small, achievable tasks.
- Use your "wasted" minutes to complete quick tasks like unpacking the dishwasher.
- Follow your cleaning system and schedule.

Procrastination

- Envision how you will feel living in a clean home. Remind yourself that not many people enjoy cleaning.
- Following the cleaning tips in this book will help you realize that cleaning doesn't have to be a difficult task.

Chapter 2

Get It Done

Now that we have established that there will never be an end to cleaning tasks around the house and that your ADHD can make these tasks seem impossible to complete, don't lose hope!

I have found the best way to clean, especially when you do have ADHD, is to do the tasks as fast as possible. This doesn't mean you should cut corners and skip areas to simply finish and tick it off your list, but rather learn my tried and tested tricks to clean in a **Fast, Simple, Efficient** way.

Allow me to teach you my cleaning philosophy: **"Get it done. It doesn't have to be perfect."** This has helped many people realize they do have what it takes to keep their spaces clean and neat.

It Doesn't Have to Be Perfect

Let's get straight into my philosophy. Your house doesn't have to be perfect. For most people, it is extremely difficult and exhausting to try and upkeep a perfectly clean home. Every time you walk in the front door, you spread dirt. Every time you cook and eat, you create dishes and dirty surfaces. Every time you put on clothes, you create laundry.

If you have small children, this task is even more difficult. The saying goes that cleaning your house with children around is the same as flossing your teeth while eating cookies. These tiny mess-makers can dirty a room that you have spent hours cleaning in less than five minutes. Whether you have young children, teenagers, young adults, partners, husbands or you live alone, your clean home is not going to last.

To find a balance in your life, family, and cleaning needs, there are two realities you should accept early on in your new cleaning journey:

1. You don't have to deep clean every time you clean your home.
2. You should create your own new idea of what a perfectly clean house means for you.

Let's get into the first reality. You might put off cleaning as you don't have the energy to move your couches or stretch muscles trying to get to the hard-to-reach (and out-of-sight) corners. There is no need to move furniture away, wash carpets, and unpack cupboards and the fridge every time you clean. If there is a mark on a wall, clean the mark off. You don't have to wash the entire wall.

You can schedule your deep cleaning for as often as you feel your home needs it, whether it is once a month, once every three months, or even once every six months. Do what you feel comfortable with, as long as it does get done. I will provide you with my exclusive resource file containing checklists for monthly, seasonal, and annual cleaning tasks. We will discuss this in more detail later.

As you create a cleaning routine and get into the rhythm of keeping your house neater, you will likely find yourself having time for deep cleaning more often. Since the rest of your house will be in better condition, the task will also not seem so overwhelming. Until then, focus on the basics and get it done.

Basics that should be done at least once a week (or every two weeks at most), include cleaning your floors (washing tiles or vacuuming carpets), cleaning your surfaces, especially in the kitchen (although surfaces should be disinfected every time you prepare food on them), and the bathroom.

We will discuss cleaning all the areas of your house in subsequent chapters, where I will include tips on what should be cleaned daily and weekly, and what you can schedule for every couple of weeks or even months.

Now, let's talk a bit about creating your own version of a perfectly clean house. Take some time to list what you believe are non-negotiables. If you need to, walk through your house, look around every room, and write down how you would want it to look. Then, add next to each item on your list what you will need to do to achieve this. Ask yourself if that is achievable. If not, you should lower your expectations to something that is realistic.

You might want to have sparkling tile floors but are not willing to sweep and wash them more than once a week. If so, your expectation might be unrealistic. You may feel tired of having toys all over your living spaces, but there might be no other places in your house for your little ones to play. Maybe adjust your expectations to allow them to play, but make packing away at a specific time of the day a non-negotiable. If you set the bar too high for yourself, you are more likely to give up on your new routine altogether.

Find ways you can get closer to your absolute ideal. Over time, you can adjust your goals and schedule to get there.

Set Cleaning Goals

Once you know what you would realistically like to achieve in your home, you can use this list of new non-negotiables to create your cleaning goals. Break your big goals (for example, not tripping over things lying on the floor as you walk in) into smaller goals. This can include:

- telling your children to pick up their toys after every play.
- picking up cushions or throws that might fall off a couch.
- throwing empty drink bottles or yogurt cups away immediately after consumption.
- packing things back where they belong as soon as you are done using them.

In general, people with ADHD often tend to focus on tasks that are less important, leaving the important tasks to weigh them down and eventually overwhelm them. Make the process less overwhelming by creating a cleaning schedule for your house. We will discuss this more in Chapter 3, but start thinking of what your schedule will likely look like.

Cleaning Is a Practice; Not a Project

Since cleaning is the one thing in your life that will be with you forever, it is good to change your mindset on how you approach it. The sooner you realize that cleaning is not a once-off occurrence, but rather a daily practice, the easier it will get.

Treating the cleaning of your house as a project gives the impression that if you work hard enough and continue at it long enough, the work will come to an end. Unfortunately, unless you have the funds to hire permanent help in cleaning your house, you will never reach the magical land where a house will stay clean. There is also no such thing as cleaning fairies who work at night. You will need to clean up after yourself.

Yes, there are bigger jobs that you might consider a project, as you may get professionals in once every couple of months to do them. These can include having your carpets or couches cleaned, your gutters and barge boards washed, and your trees felled. These hired professionals are likely the closest you will get to cleaning fairies.

The rest of your cleaning jobs should be considered smaller tasks (remember the smaller goals I advised you to create) that you do consistently. Cleaning should be a daily practice, where you schedule yourself tasks to do every day. This will

---

help to make the tasks less overwhelming, and if you know exactly what to do, they will likely be easier to start and complete.

Time Your Tasks

Another thing that can help you start your chores more easily is knowing exactly how long it will take to complete them. Many times, tasks are put off as you think they will take a long time to complete. Knowing that a specific task will only take you 15 minutes and not an hour will increase the chances of actually starting the chore. You will feel more motivated to get it done, as you will soon be able to go over to do things that you enjoy.

This is why it is important to time how long it takes to complete a specific task. Write this down, so you can use this when planning your tasks. You will be surprised to find that, on average, unloading a dishwasher only takes three to five minutes. A big load of laundry takes, at most, 20 minutes to fold and pack away.

You might be surprised at how quickly you can complete these tasks. At first, I was too. But, once you change your mindset about this, you won't dread starting these tasks anymore.

Chapter Summary

Always remember that your cleaning job doesn't have to be perfect every time. The most important thing is to just get it done. Let's recap on how you can speed up your cleaning routine:

- You don't have to deep clean every time you clean your home.
- Create your own ideal of what a perfectly clean house means for you.
- Set your cleaning goals by breaking big tasks into small, achievable tasks.
- Remember that cleaning is an ongoing practice, not a project you can complete and forget about.
- Time how long it takes to complete a task. Knowing exactly how long it will take to do something, will help you to realize how many tasks you can actually get done in only 30 minutes.

Chapter 3

Clean the Fast, Simple, Efficient Way

You have now created your cleaning goals. You have thought about what would be realistically achievable in your circumstances. Remember, it doesn't have to be absolutely perfect. Just get it done!

You understand that cleaning is an ongoing practice. You can't clean today and believe your home will magically keep itself clean. You need to keep at it. You might have already started timing yourself to complete tasks. I am sure you were amazed at how little time you actually need to do some of them.

Now, let's go over to the next step in your new cleaning journey. We will discuss different strategies you can implement in your new routine to help you clean the **Fast, Simple, Efficient way.**

Cyclone Cleaning

The best way I have found to clean **Fast, Simply, and Efficiently** is to start every cleaning task with a quick cyclone clean. First, decide on a timeframe for this. Cyclone cleaning is meant to be a fast and furious tidying up. Five minutes may be all you will need to do this.

Once you have decided on a timeframe, set a timer to let you know when you have reached your time limit. Take a box or a basket and put everything in there that doesn't belong in the area you are wanting to clean. Don't waste time wondering how something got in that specific room, or even why you bought an item. You can waste time solving these mysteries on another occasion. The purpose of a cyclone clean is not to declutter your space, but simply to tidy up and clear the surfaces that need to be cleaned. Decluttering is a job for later.

Once you have boxed the things that were laying around, you will be able to clean a lot more quickly and easily. There won't be things in the way when you want to dust or wipe counters. You will also not feel overwhelmed by the number of things you will need to sort out.

Cleaning Caddy

Make cleaning as easy and effortless as possible for yourself by creating personalized cleaning caddies or boxes for different areas of the house. Keep a caddy permanently in the bathroom, another one in the kitchen, and create a third one you can carry around with you when you are cleaning the other zones in the house.

Make sure you have everything you will need for every zone in your home in its respective caddy. As we discuss cleaning every zone in the house, I will include a checklist of tools and products you will need in your caddy.

Having your caddy ready to go will result in you not having to run up and down to get things while you are cleaning. This will help you to stay focused on what you are doing. Keep a notepad and a garbage bag in your caddy. This way you can make notes of all the products that must be replaced, and be able to discard the empty containers. You can also throw any dust you sweep up or other refuse straight into these bags.

Daily Five

When you start to think about cleaning your space, you will realize there will always be tasks you need to do daily. Look around your house at what needs to be done.

These tasks can include making the beds, doing dishes, emptying the dishwasher (remember, it takes less than five minutes to do), doing laundry, straightening the cushions, and wiping down countertops. There might be other unique tasks for your home, such as cleaning pet bowls or cat litter trays, and picking up toys.

Once you have decided on your five daily tasks, make sure to put them within sight as reminders. Try to do these tasks as quickly as you can, so you get in the habit of getting them done. Remember, it doesn't have to be perfect all the time. Completing your five tasks every day will help you feel a lot more organized.

Do tasks you can do in the morning (such as making beds) as soon as possible after you get up. If you start your day by ticking something off your list within five minutes of getting up, you will feel more positive about the rest of your tasks.

An example of my daily five is:

- make the beds
- do the dishes or load and unload the dishwasher
- clean the kitchen sink
- wipe down countertops
- clean cat litter trays and pet bowls

Zone Cleaning

When you look at the different spaces in your home that need cleaning, it is easy to be overwhelmed by the amount of work to be done. You might feel like you don't have the time or energy to spend hours cleaning. The more you put it off, the bigger the job gets, and the more overwhelmed you feel by it.

Make this mammoth task smaller by breaking your home up into different zones. This is called zone cleaning. The purpose of this is to clean smaller zones at a time so that you never spend more than 20 or 30 minutes in a zone.

The first thing you need to do is divide your home up into zones. Look at how long you usually spend cleaning each specific room. Bathrooms and kitchens tend to have a lot more areas that need a thorough cleaning.

Once you know how much time you need per area, look at what rooms you can group together in one zone. If you have an open-plan living and dining space, this can fall into one zone. Aim at creating at most five cleaning zones in your home—I will explain the reason for the five zones in the section below.

An example of how a typical home can be grouped is as follows:

- **Zone 1**: living spaces (living room, dining room, family room, etc.)
- **Zone 2**: kitchen
- **Zone 3**: bathroom(s)/laundry
- **Zone 4**: bedrooms
- **Zone 5**: entrance, front porch, veranda, hallways, den, and home office

After you have decided on your different cleaning zones, you are ready to start. Get all the tools you will need: your cyclone cleaning box or basket, your cleaning caddy, and a timer. Start by doing a five to ten-minute cyclone clean. Once the timer goes off, put your cyclone cleaning box away and set your timer again for 30 minutes. You might be surprised at how many minutes will still be left on the timer after you are done cleaning.

Make a note of this. These extra minutes left on the clock after every clean add up. After a month you might easily have two hours or even more of "saved" time. Use this time to reward yourself for cleaning the **Fast, Simple, Efficient** way.

Let's say, for example, you have two hours and six minutes saved; go do something that you really enjoy for that exact amount of time. Enjoy the satisfaction you will experience knowing you have earned this time and that you will have a clean house to come home to.

Cleaning Schedules

Before you start daydreaming about how you will spend your saved time, first we need to go back to how to implement zone cleaning in your home. Simply dividing your home into zones will not make you magically jump into action.

The next step is to create your own cleaning schedule. To avoid getting overwhelmed by your cleaning, I find it extremely helpful to schedule one zone only for a day. This means that, apart from tasks that you do need to do daily (the daily five), you will only spend around 30 minutes a day cleaning. And, since you will do a bit every day, your house will constantly get clean without overwhelming you or working you into a sweat.

Decide how scheduling these zones will fit in best with your lifestyle. If you often have people over on a weekend, you might want to leave the living areas and bathrooms for later in the week, so that they are still clean when your guests arrive.

An example of a cleaning schedule can be as follows:

- **Monday**: bedrooms
- **Tuesday**: kitchen
- **Wednesday**: entrance, front porch, veranda, hallways, den, and home office
- **Thursday**: living spaces (living room, dining room, family room, etc.)
- **Friday**: bathrooms/laundry

If your space is small enough and you would prefer to keep your Fridays open, you can look at only creating four cleaning zones in your house. Just make sure that cleaning those four zones will not take too long, as this might demotivate you. Adapt this practice to suit your personal needs, home, and lifestyle.

Keep two days of the week free for catch-ups on tasks you might have missed, doing extras such as deep cleaning, organizing and decluttering, or simply relaxing and enjoying your clean space. On one of these days at the end of each month, you can use the time you have saved cleaning to reward yourself with something you really enjoy.

There are many ways of creating your cleaning schedule. You might want to get your creative juices flowing with pretty designs and bright-colored highlighters. Be careful of using this as a trap to procrastinate on what is actually important. We are talking about creating a schedule, not a piece of art. My exclusive, free resource contains templates for cleaning schedules, which you can customize to suit your needs.

Learn to Delegate

Once you have created your cleaning schedule, don't keep it hidden in a folder on your computer or stashed away at the back of your closet. Rather put your schedule and zones up somewhere in the house where you will not only be reminded of what needs to be done, but so that other family members or people who share the space, will also know what should be cleaned on different days.

When cleaning, keep in mind that unless you live alone, you are not the only one making the house dirty. Therefore, you should not necessarily have to be the only one responsible for keeping it neat and clean. Try to share the workload where you can. If the other people who share the space help to clean, they are more likely to try and keep it clean for longer.

Give everyone ownership of a specific aspect of cleaning. To do this, you can create a list of tasks for each person or member of the family for that zone. If the space is not big enough for everyone to work in at the same time, assign them tasks in other zones to do while you focus on the zone of the day.

If you have children, keep the tasks age-appropriate. Children can be brilliant at cyclone cleaning the zone scheduled for the next day and taking dirty clothes to the laundry. That way, you will likely spend a lot less time during your cyclone clean when you get to that zone, saving you more time to spend doing something you enjoy at the end of the month.

Don't Delay

If you are wondering where you will find the time to do a bit of cleaning every day (even though you will only need half an hour daily), here's a handy tip for you: Don't delay. If you work from home or stay at home then get started as soon as you can. If you can do your cleaning earlier in the day, you will be able to tackle other things later, without worrying about having to clean. If you work outside the home, then try and get straight into it as soon as you get home. Get it done as quickly as you can before you fall into the trap of sitting down.

Many people believe they first need to catch a breather and relax when they come home. However, you will likely find yourself a couple of hours later still on the couch. Not many people will get up at 8:00 p.m. to start cleaning.

You might even find yourself not being able to truly relax if you first sit down, as you will have your cleaning task of the day hanging over your head the whole time. This will not be the case if you clean immediately as you come home. Of course, everyone's situation is different, but the point I'm trying to make is don't delay or put it off. Get your cleaning done as soon as you can.

Make It Fun

If you really dislike cleaning, try your best to make it as fun as possible. One way of doing this is by turning your cleaning into a speed race. Time yourself completing a task and every time you need to do this task again, see if you can beat your previous score. Remember, cheaters aren't winners, so do this without cutting corners.

If doing a speed race is not up your alley, think of other ways you can make cleaning more bearable. Play music and dance while you clean, listen to a podcast or audiobook, or phone a friend that you know likes to talk for a long time. Continue talking until the conversation is over. Another way you can motivate yourself to clean is by inviting guests over. Knowing other people will see the mess you live in can give you the energy boost you need to get everything in place.

Chapter Summary

Get your cleaning goals done the **Fast, Simple, Efficient** way by following these steps:

- Start every cleaning job with a quick five-minute cyclone clean.
- Make cleaning caddies for the different spaces in your home. Keep one permanently in the bathroom, another one in the kitchen, and then one to carry around with you while you clean.
- Divide your home up into cleaning zones. When you clean, only concentrate on the zone you are busy with and forget about the rest.
- Create your cleaning schedule by dedicating one day per week to each zone of the home. Doing a little every day will keep your home clean and the cleaning tasks less overwhelming.
- Unless you live by yourself, delegate some of the cleaning tasks to your family or the people you live with. You don't have to do everything by yourself.
- Decide on your daily five tasks that must be completed every day. Do these tasks as quickly as you can.
- Don't delay. Get your zone of the day cleaned as soon as you can.
- Try to make cleaning as fun as possible. Put on music, listen to an audiobook or podcast or challenge yourself to a speed race.

Chapter 4

Clean Efficiently

After you have divided your home into cleaning zones, scheduled these zones, and gotten your baskets ready for doing cyclone cleaning, you are almost ready to start cleaning your spaces. Before we get there, it is important to first discuss some cleaning techniques.

You might think this is unnecessary, as you have been cleaning all your life, so you know how to clean. Through the way you have been cleaning in the past, you might have created double work for yourself. You may wonder why your surfaces never look clean, as there are always little streaks after you wipe them. It may even be that you don't know how to use products properly, as they never work as well as promised on the label.

If that sounds like your life, this is for you. Learning these techniques will make your cleaning process **Fast, Simple, and Efficient**.

Straightening Up

Many people would love clutter-free surfaces in their homes, as it creates the impression of a clean area and gives you ample space to work in, for example, a kitchen. However, in some instances, it can be impossible to avoid having things placed on your surfaces or countertops. Unfortunately, no matter how much you clean a surface, it can still look messy if you are not careful about how you place these items on your counters.

If that is the case in your home, make sure you place them as neatly as possible. Line them up as far back on your surface as possible, and put them in a straight line, or group them together. This way it will be clear that they are meant to be there and not just clutter that you haven't had time to put away yet.

The key is always to keep any horizontal surface in your home as clean and clutter-free as possible, and to place the things that you need to have out as neatly as possible. Revisit these surfaces often to make sure there aren't more items on these surfaces than what is absolutely necessary. Over time, you might even find the perfect place to put these items out of sight.

Get the Microfibers

Many people have numerous different cleaning rags and paper towels they use to do their jobs. Although it is good to have a cloth dedicated to a specific area such as the bathroom, you don't have to go all out when buying them.

A simple microfiber cloth will do the trick on most surfaces, as it will not scratch your surfaces or leave streaks. These cloths are even great for dusting areas. Even though paper towels are great for many different cleaning jobs and absorbing spills, they are tree-based products that can cause minor scratches on some surfaces.

Follow a Path

It is good to follow a specific routine when you clean, as it will keep you focused on what you are doing, what you have done, and what you still need to do. Otherwise, you might forget what you have cleaned already and what you must still do. This might lead you to clean the same surfaces more than once, or get so frazzled, confused, and overwhelmed that you stop halfway through.

A good routine to follow is cleaning from top to bottom, left to right. When you clean the top surfaces of your space, such as high cupboards or walls, dust will fall down. If you have already cleaned, for example, your floors, the dust will fall on your clean floors, resulting in you having to clean them again. If you clean the top parts of your space first, it won't matter if the dust falls on your lower surfaces or floors, as you will get to those areas last.

Moving in your space from left to right (or right to left, if that is what you prefer) will help you to keep track of what you have cleaned already. You will never miss an area if you follow this cleaning rule. Even if you are interrupted, you will know exactly where to start once you come back to your task.

Let It Dwell

Have you ever thrown cleaning products away thinking they don't work? If yes, did you give these products enough time to do their job? Or did you simply spray them on, and wipe them off again?

If you nodded in agreement to the last question, this one is for you. Cleaning products need time to do their job. They need to break up and lift the dirt that is sitting on your surfaces. If these products have antibacterial agents, they need even more time to kill the bacteria living in your spaces.

This is why it is so important to allow these products to sit on your surfaces for about five to ten minutes after you spray them on. Use this time while you wait to do other tasks in your cleaning zone. For example, if you are cleaning the kitchen, you can spray your surfaces and then unload the dishwasher, do the dishes, or start a load of laundry while you let the product sit.

When you are ready to start wiping these areas off, start at the spot you sprayed first and work from there, top to bottom, left to right. You will see that if you give your products a bit of time to dwell, your surfaces will clean more easily and you will get the great results you desire.

Start Gentle

If you have not allowed your cleaning products to dwell in the past, you might believe the gentler products don't work well. As a result, you have likely come into the habit of grabbing the strongest cleaning products to do simple jobs.

Strong cleaning products release a lot of chemicals into the air, which can be harmful to you, your family, and your pets, if you have them. Medical studies have proven that these chemicals can contribute to allergic reactions, headaches, asthma, and chronic respiratory problems (American Lung Association, n.d.).

Many times, you might find that if you use the most gentle product and allow it enough time to sit on the dirt, the product will work. If not, gradually work your way up in the strength of your product. However, if your surfaces are very greasy or if your cake tin has leaked batter in your oven that is now burned to the bottom, you might have to reach for the strong stuff.

If there are so many cleaning products on the market that your head spins trying to decide what to buy, you might want to consider making your own products. Homemade or DIY cleaning products are better for your health and the environment, and are much cheaper to use.

You can make your own cleaning product for basically any job in the house, from cleaning the toilet to the dishwasher. I will provide you with a list of recipes you can easily make at home in my exclusive resource file. We will discuss this file in more detail later.

Crouch Down

When you clean your countertops in your kitchen, for example, you spray your product, let it dwell, and then wipe it off. The result is a perfectly clean counter, right? Well, that is not always the case. If you have appliances on your counters that you do not move away every time you clean, you might be shocked to see what hides underneath there.

Coming back to "it doesn't have to be perfect and you don't have to do a deep clean every time you clean your space," the same goes for your counters. You don't have to lift and move heavy appliances all the time. To determine if it is necessary to move an appliance, you can simply crouch down so you are facing the counter at eye level, and look for any crumbs or dust hiding underneath.

If you haven't moved an appliance in a while, you might be shocked to see the state of your counters when you look from that viewpoint. If you can't see any crumbs underneath and you have cleaned underneath the appliance a week or two before that, you can skip moving it for another week if you like and get the rest of the zone clean.

Your Wiping Pattern

Everyone has their own way of wiping walls or counters. Some do parallel lines, while others wipe in circles. Doing the circle pattern can be problematic, as you might spread more dirt that is on your cloth than cleaning the actual surface. This often results in a surface with streaks and marks on them, which you will have to wipe again to get off.

Avoid this by wiping your surfaces in a parallel zigzag or S-pattern. After you have sprayed your surface and let the product sit for a couple of minutes, start in a corner of your surface and wipe with your cloth in a straight line across. Once you get to the end, bring the cloth slightly down, and wipe it back. Continue this until your entire surface has been wiped.

By doing this, you will avoid spreading dirt over surfaces that have already been cleaned. Your surfaces will have a lot fewer wiping streaks and marks, so you will not have to go back and clean them again.

Chapter Summary

Using the right techniques while cleaning will help you to get the job done **Fast, Simply, and Efficiently**:

- Straighten up and keep areas as clutter-free as possible.
- Use microfiber cloths, as they are super absorbent and will not leave streaks.
- Move around the zone you are cleaning in a clockwise direction. Remember to always clean top to bottom.
- Let your cleaning products dwell for at least five minutes before wiping the surface.
- Use a gentle cleaning product first and only if that doesn't work, try something stronger.
- Crouch down to check how clean a surface is.
- Use an 'S' or zigzag pattern when cleaning.

Chapter 5

The Living Areas

Now that you have learned some proven techniques that will make your cleaning more efficient, and maybe even have realized some cleaning mistakes you might have made in the past, it is time to get into cleaning the different zones in your home.

The first zone we will look at is the living areas. These are generally areas that get a lot of foot traffic, and therefore, need cleaning and tidying up regularly. This zone includes areas like the living room, formal lounge if you have one, dining room, and family room.

The living areas of your home are usually filled with big and bulky furniture, such as sofas, chairs, tables, cabinets, and electronics, such as a television. Remember that you do not have to move the furniture around for a deep clean every time you clean. As long as you get to the hard-to-reach areas underneath or behind the couches every now and again, you can concentrate your efforts on the areas you can see.

The Fast, Simple, Efficient System

As we have mentioned above, your living areas can easily become a mess of clutter lying around, not even mentioning what may be hiding behind your couches. The hidden dirt lurking behind furniture is not of any concern when you do a quick clean using the **Fast, Simple, Efficient Cleaning System**:

- Take a basket and do a quick cyclone clean. Put everything that doesn't belong in the living area in the basket, take any dirty dishes to the kitchen, and put everything that can be thrown away in the garbage bag.
- Once you have freed your horizontal surfaces from clutter, take a dry microfiber cloth and dust off all your surfaces.
- Now, take your all-purpose cleaner and spray those surfaces. As you walk around the room, be on the lookout for anything else that needs urgent attention. You might see a mark on a wall or your windowsill might have some dust. Deal with this now.
- Put all the cushions or throws neatly back in place.
- By the time you have done your rounds and sorted your cushions, your cleaning product will have had time to dwell. Wipe those surfaces quickly. Once the surfaces are dry, put back everything that belongs on them.
- Now it is time to get to your floors. We will discuss cleaning your floors in detail below, but the most important thing is to start in the furthest corner and

work your way back to the entrance of the room. That way you avoid walking on your freshly cleaned floors.

- Just like that, your living areas will look professionally cleaned in under 30 minutes. As much as you might want to pat yourself on the back, first sort out all the clutter lying in the basket. This might include dirty clothes (take them to the laundry or put in a laundry hamper), toys (to the kids' room), and stationery (to the home office or area you keep them).
- Take your cyclone cleaning garbage bag to your garbage bin, and pack your dirty dishes in the dishwasher, or give it a quick hand wash.

Lastly and maybe most importantly, be impressed with how fast and efficiently you can clean.

Let's Do Some Deep Cleaning

Once in a while, you will have to do a deep clean. This, however, doesn't have to take hours to do. There are many hacks to make even your deep cleaning **Fast, Simple and Efficient.**

Dusting

When it comes to dusting, it is important to remember it is a combination of everything you have in your home, from your fabrics, your skin, your pets, and everything else. When this fine mist becomes wet, it can get sticky and become a lot harder to clean off. This is why it is always important to dust with a dry microfiber cloth first before you use a spray cleaner.

Spread your cloth open, and then fold it in quarters. This way you essentially have eight clean cloths to work with. As the first quarter of your cloth gets dirty, you simply use the other side of the folded cloth. Once both sides are dirty, fold it open once, and make another quarter with the dirty sides in. Use these two new clean sides to wipe your furniture or surfaces and, when they are also dirty, open the entire cloth, and start folding your quarters again with the dirty sides in.

Remove each item (pot plants, photo frames, or ornaments) from the surface you want to dust and wipe the entire surface in one quick move. Then, dust all your items off on the floor before you place them back on your surface.

If you choose to use a feather duster, remember that these tools can actually spread the dust more if you are not careful. Take the duster in your hand and move it from one side of the area you wish to dust to the other side as quickly as possible. Then, bring it low to the ground and give it a quick tap to allow the dust to fall from the duster to the floor.

After you have dusted, leave the room for a couple of minutes for the dust to settle before you start to clean your floors.

Sofas and Other Soft Furniture

The deep cleaning of your soft surfaces, such as sofas, should be done at least once a year, and it is best left to professionals with specialized equipment. However, that doesn't mean that for the rest of the year you simply just leave it to gather dust and brew bacteria.

To clean your sofas, you can use a soft-bristle brush to brush off any loose dirt on the couches. This brush will not damage the material but can help you reach a bit deeper into the corners between the seats and the back or armrests. Once you have brushed your couches, vacuum them to remove as much dust and dirt as possible.

If there are marks on your sofas, use a wet cloth to clean them off after you have vacuumed. If plain water doesn't remove the stains, you can use a fabric stain remover. Always make sure you use bleach-free products on your upholstery to not cause more stains.

Since soft surfaces are known to collect bacteria, they can start to smell. If this is the case and it is still months before your next professional clean, sprinkle baking soda over your couches. Let this rest for about 15 minutes, and vacuum it up.

Remember to clean any cushions or throws you might have on your couches regularly. These can also be vacuumed when you clean your couches, or you can put them in the washing machine or take them to your local laundromat.

Television

There are not a lot of things as irritating as seeing fingermarks on your television when you are binge-watching your favorite show. You might not know how to clean it, because the last thing you want to do is cause damage by using a cleaning product on it or leave streaks from wiping your screen.

The only form of liquid you should ever attempt to use on your television is distilled water and only a drop or two on a microfiber cloth. You should never spray this water directly onto the screen because if the water drips down and enters the binding at the bottom of the screen, you will likely have to throw your television in the trash.

Before you use the water, first try to dry clean your screen. If that doesn't work, take a deep breath, and exhale through your mouth directly onto the screen where the mark is. This will create enough moisture on the screen to clean it, but not enough to damage your television. Now, wipe it gently with either a microfiber cloth or an optical cloth (those little cloths that are usually used to clean glasses).

Always make sure your television has been turned off for at least a couple of minutes to cool off before you clean it. Otherwise, you run the risk of damaging the screen when you wipe it. When you do wipe your screen, be careful to never apply too much pressure. Just give it a very light and gentle wipe.

Wooden Furniture: Coffee and Dining Tables

When it comes to solid wooden furniture, such as coffee, side, and dining tables, it is best to first determine if these are finished or unfinished wood. Do a quick test by putting a drop of water on the furniture. If it absorbs into the wood, it is unfinished. If it beads on top of the furniture, it is finished wood.

To clean your unfinished wooden furniture, only use a dry microfiber cloth to wipe up any dust. For finished wooden furniture, spray a bit of plain water on the furniture and wipe it off with your microfiber cloth. This will reduce any streaks on your furniture, and give it the shine it wants.

Furniture polish is not always necessary to use, and depending on the type of wood your furniture was made of, it can even make your furniture look dull. If you want to use polish, first confirm what type of wood you are dealing with, and get the polish that was specifically made for that type of wood.

If there are watermarks on your furniture, you don't have to rush to the store for a specialized cleaner or oil to repair it. You can simply apply mayonnaise on the spot, leave it overnight, and wipe it off the next morning.

Blinds

Blinds can be tricky to clean; so tricky, in fact, that many people skip over this step and end up never cleaning them properly, or getting professionals in to do this job once a year. It doesn't have to be that difficult. You also don't need fancy equipment to do this. An old sock and rubbing alcohol in a spray bottle will do.

First, dust your blinds to try and get as much dust off the blinds as possible. Alternatively, you can vacuum your blinds to remove the dust. If you do this regularly, you only need to do a deeper cleaning of your blinds every couple of months.

For this deeper clean, flip the blinds so that they lay flat to one side. Put the sock over one hand, and take the spray bottle in the other. Spray the blinds well, and wipe them with the socked hand. Once you are done, turn the blinds to lay to the other side, and repeat the process.

Walls

All the walls in your home will need to be washed from time to time; however, this is most definitely not needed every time you do a deep clean. If you see a spot on the wall, it also doesn't mean you necessarily have to wash the entire wall.

Baking soda and a sponge can serve as a magical eraser for spots on your wall. Throw some baking soda into one hand, dip the corner of a damp sponge into the baking soda, and use this to wipe any mark, fingerprint, or grease spots off any wall. Once you see the spot is gone, use a damp microfiber cloth to wipe the baking soda off.

Floors

The way you clean the floors in your living spaces will largely depend on the type of floors you have: carpets, tiles, wooden floors, laminate floors, or luxury vinyl. However, they all come down to the same technique: starting from the furthest corner of your room and working your way back. This will avoid you having to walk over your clean floors.

When it comes to vacuuming your carpets, always make sure you are using the right attachments for the job at hand. As with sofas, carpets can get very smelly, so you can sprinkle some baking soda all over your carpets, leave it to dwell for about 15 minutes, and then vacuum it up. This also helps to loosen carpet fibers, helping you clean more effectively.

When it comes to hard floors—tiles, hardwood, laminate, and luxury vinyl—it is important to first sweep or vacuum the floors before you mop them. This way you remove all dirt and dust, resulting in a cleaner finish.

You can spray your tiles with your all-purpose cleaner of choice, leave it to dwell for a bit, and then simply go over your floors with a mop. If there are areas with harder dirt that are more difficult to clean, spray some more product and leave it a bit longer before you mop it up.

When it comes to hardwood, laminate, and luxury vinyl floors, it is important to never use a steam mop, as it can damage your floors. Always mop in the direction of the grains of your floors to reduce any visible streaks on your floors.

Be careful about using cleaning products on these floors, as the wrong products can cause damage. If there are any liquid spills on these floors, make sure you clean them up immediately. Also make sure your mop is only slightly damp, as too much moisture on this type of floor can cause the wood or laminate to expand.

Home Odors

Many areas of the house can often be filled with sometimes funky odors. This is particularly the case for living areas that get a lot of foot traffic. If this is the case for your home, it is important to first find the source of the odor in your house. If you just try and mask the smell by bringing in diffusers and other air fresheners, the odor will still be there, even though it might be less.

However, if you find the source and treat it, it won't be necessary to spend extra money on different air fresheners. If you have pets in the house, they can often be the cause of unwanted smells. As we have mentioned, soft surfaces such as sofas, ottomans, pillows, linen, and carpets can also be the culprits.

If you can't find the problem area, there are easy steps you can take to reduce the smells in the house. One of these steps is making sure you have good quality airflow in your home. Open the windows in your home as often as you can. Nothing beats getting natural fresh air into your home.

Air purifiers can help to clean the air in your home. You can add essential oils to these purifiers to deodorize your home if you feel the need. Just be careful if you have pets, as some essential oils can be toxic to animals. My exclusive, free resource file contains lists of essential oils that are toxic to dogs and cats, as well as safe ones you can use around your pets.

Vacuuming your soft surfaces (and hard floors) regularly can help in removing the dust that can cause stuffy smells in your home.

You can also look at using products to absorb odors in your space. This does not need to break the bank. You can place a bowl with white vinegar, baking soda, or activated charcoal in the spaces where you struggle with odors.

Chapter Summary

To make sure you have the right tools and cleaning products to clean your living areas, here is a checklist of what you need to clean your living room.

In Your Caddy:

- garbage bag
- all-purpose cleaner
- distilled water
- rubbing alcohol (for blinds)
- glass cleaner (if necessary)
- microfiber cloths
- soft-bristle brush
- an old sock (if you have blinds)
- baking soda, vinegar, or activated charcoal (for odors)

Extra Equipment:

- vacuum cleaner
- broom and mop (if you have hard floors)
- Basket/box for cyclone cleaning

Chapter 6
The Kitchen

The kitchen is often called the heart of the home, and can often be the heart of dirt, messes, and bacteria as well. This is also the area where you will bring all your grocery/ shopping bags, which can result in more bacteria entering your house.

This is why it is important to keep your kitchen as clean as possible, particularly the countertops where you will be preparing food. However, there is more to cleaning the kitchen than just wiping countertops. Tasks in the kitchen will include cleaning dishes, pots, cutting boards, and appliances such as microwaves, ovens, stovetops, and fridges.

Luckily, these don't have to be cleaned every time you have your kitchen scheduled for a quick clean.

The Fast, Simple, Efficient System

Doing a quick clean of your kitchen can really be very fast, especially if you take care to wipe your counters after every use. Let's look at the steps to cleaning the kitchen the **Fast, Simple, Efficient** way:

- Take your cyclone cleaning basket and garbage bag and put everything cluttering your surfaces away. If the ketchup bottle is still standing on the counter from last night's French fries, pack it away where it belongs. Make sure you get your countertops as empty as possible. Put any dirty dishes straight into the dishwasher, or stack them in the sink.
- Take your dry microfiber cloth and dust everything that needs some attention. You will soon come to realize where dust likes to sit in your kitchen. If you see dust or dirt in any other area of your kitchen, take care of it now. Don't worry if the dust or crumbs fall from the countertops to the floor. It is for this reason that you always clean your floors last.
- Take your all-purpose cleaner and spray all your countertops. If there are marks on any of your cupboards, or you feel it is time to clean them as well, spray and let your product dwell. Don't forget about the cupboard and fridge door handles.
- If you need to handwash your dishes, do it now and clean the counters around your sink.
- Start to wipe your surfaces from top to bottom, working in a clockwise or left-to-right path. When wiping, remember your 'S' or a zigzag pattern.
- Finish the kitchen by cleaning your floors. This can include first sweeping or vacuuming the floors, spraying all-purpose cleaners on your floors, and then mopping them clean. Start in the furthest corner and work your way back to the entrance to the kitchen.

Within 30 minutes, your kitchen will be ready for guests popping by for a cup of coffee.

Let's Do Some Deep Cleaning

As much as doing a quick clean of the kitchen can be a super-fast job, deep cleaning this room can easily overwhelm you, as there is so much to do. Remember that you don't have to do it all at the same time. As you get used to keeping your kitchen neat, you will spend less time doing your weekly cleaning, so you might feel up to doing a deeper clean sooner than you think.

There are many cleaning products available to use, and many recipes in my exclusive resource file you can make yourself at home. Keep an eye out in this book on how to get access to my resource file.

Let's take deep cleaning your kitchen step-by-step and discuss each section or appliance in your kitchen.

Cupboards

Many people forget to clean the cupboards in their kitchen. This is not something you will need to do during every clean, but it is good to get to every couple of weeks. Be mindful of what material your kitchen cupboards are made of so you don't cause any damage using a specific cleaning product on them. Otherwise, you can play it safe by using a combination of dish soap and water, or your favorite all-purpose cleaner. If your normal cleaner or soap is not strong enough to remove tough pieces of dirt, you can look at using an enzyme cleaner.

Remember to work from top to bottom, left to right. This means you will spray the entire cupboard at once, but start wiping it from the top to the bottom. If your cupboard has a lot of grooves in them (especially on the front-facing doors), use a cleaning toothbrush to clean it properly.

Countertops

When it comes to cleaning your countertops, it is important to first determine what they are made of. On laminate tops, you can use pretty much any cleaning product you want. They tend to be very durable. Be careful of bleach products, as they can leave permanent marks on laminate tops. Natural stone tops can be trickier, as some products can affect the appearance of the stone. If you have stone tops, determine what stones they are made of, and then make sure your cleaner won't damage the stone.

In general, most people prefer to use antibacterial disinfectant products to clean their kitchens. This is due to the potential bacteria that can spread as you bring your groceries in after a shopping trip and while cooking.

Make sure your countertops are cleared of any clutter. Spray the surfaces with your cleaner of choice and let it dwell for five to ten minutes. Then wipe your counters off in a 'S' or zigzag pattern, making sure you don't miss a spot.

Microwave

This appliance can often be filled with big messes on the inside, and often without you even realizing it. It is due to the food "exploding" inside the microwave as you warm it up. Due to the constant heat from using the microwave, the food residues inside it can stick to the appliance like glue.

This is why it is always good to cover any food you are heating up. However, these covers are not always mess-proof and residues of food can still end up all over the inside of your appliance. If you are not super proactive about cleaning your microwave after every use, you are bound to have to do a deep clean from time to time.

To do this, place a microwaveable bowl filled with water and sliced lemon in the appliance, and switch it on for about three to five minutes. Once it is done, take the bowl out (carefully, as it will be hot) and use a microfiber cloth to clean the inside thoroughly. The dirt should come off easily.

Also, don't forget to clean the outside of your microwave. Be careful not to spray your cleaning products straight onto the electronic touchpad of your appliance. Instead, spray your product on your cloth, and then wipe your appliance clean.

Dishes

Doing the dishes is one of those cleaning jobs that seems to never end. The moment you think you have done them all, you may walk around the house and find more, or you may pour yourself a glass of water, creating more dishes.

Even if you have a dishwasher, there will always be some dishes that you will have to wash by hand. Make this job as easy as possible for yourself by investing in the right tools for the job. These include rubber gloves, a non-scratch sponge or scourer, and maybe a dish wand.

Wash your dishes in order of greasiness. Start with the least greasy dishes (normally glasses and other drinkware), then move to your cutlery, plates, and bowls, and then end off with your greasy pots and pans.

Pots

You may feel so demotivated by burned food in a pot that you want to throw the whole pot out than stand hours scrubbing and cleaning. There are, however, some super easy ways to remove even the blackest of burn marks in a pot.

Put water in the pot, and add either some baking soda or vinegar to it. Put it on the stove and bring it to boil for a couple of minutes. Then, throw the boiling water mixture out, and most (if not all) of the burn marks will be gone. Repeat this process if necessary. You can also use a wooden spoon to rub the baking soda on burn marks if they don't come loose by just boiling the water.

Alternatively, take some tin foil, crumple it up into a ball, add dish soap and some water, and use the tin foil to scrub the pot. This will work much more effectively than any kitchen sponge or scourer you might have used in the past.

Cutting Boards

Cutting boards should be cleaned after every use and need a deeper cleaning regularly. Since you cut your food directly on them, bacteria can often build on them, and even with a good scrub, you might not be able to clean thoroughly between the grooves made by previous cuts on wooden and plastic cutting boards.

To clean in between these grooves, use clean hydrogen peroxide. Spray this straight onto your cutting boards and leave it to sit for five to ten minutes. Then, wash them thoroughly using soap and water. After they have been washed, dry them immediately.

Marks on Glasses

To remove marks and streaks on glasses, you don't need a lot of elbow grease. All you need to do is change the way you rinse your glassware after you have washed them.

Wash your glasses in warm soapy water. Then, instead of rinsing them in plain water, add some white vinegar to your water. This will help to break down any residue that might still be on your glasses, giving them a shining look free from streaks and marks. After you have rinsed your glasses, dry them properly using a microfiber cloth.

Sink

Once you have finished washing your dishes, don't forget to also wash your kitchen sink. First, spray it thoroughly with your choice of all-purpose cleaner. Then, sprinkle some baking soda in the sink and give it a couple of minutes to settle. Next, take your cleaning toothbrush and make sure you scrub in all the little corners of the sink to clean the hidden dirt out properly.

After you are done with the toothbrush, take a scourer sponge and use the scouring pad to rub the baking soda around your sink, cleaning the entire sink. This helps to lift up any grease that is stuck in your sink after doing the dishes. Rinse it out well, and then dry your sink using a microfiber cloth.

Dishwasher

From time to time, you will need to clean the inside of your dishwasher to optimize its cleaning ability and reduce any odors that might accumulate in it. If you want to give it a quick clean, make sure it is empty and sprinkle baking soda at the bottom of it. Leave it for a couple of hours, then switch the machine on.

Once the dishwasher has filled with some hot water, open it and add a cup of white vinegar to it. Then close it and let it run a cycle.

If you want to give it a deeper clean, remove the cutlery tray and bottom rack and spray some all-purpose cleaner all over the inside of the machine. Then make a paste of baking soda and dish soap and use your cleaning toothbrush to scrub this paste on all the areas that need cleaning. Once you start, you will likely find many spots around the door of the dishwasher that need cleaning. Leave this to dwell for a couple of minutes before you rinse it off.

Next, remove the filter from the dishwasher and let it soak in hot, soapy water. Once it has soaked for a while, give it a bit of a scrub, rinse it off, and place it back in your machine.

Blender

Many people believe cleaning a blender is a massive job. So big, in fact, that they avoid using their blenders as they don't want to go through the effort of cleaning it. However, with just following a couple of easy steps, your blender can practically clean itself. After you use it, rinse your blender out to remove as many pieces of food as possible. Add a squirt of dish soap and fill it about halfway with water.

Put the blender back on its base, and switch it on for a couple of minutes. Then, rinse it out again and allow it to dry. It can be that easy!

Toaster

A toaster is an appliance that can easily make a big mess if it is not cleaned regularly. It can lead to crumbs all over your surfaces. Most toasters have a little drawer called a crumb tray at the bottom that you can take out to remove most of the crumbs from the inside of the appliance. Always hold the toaster over your sink or dustbin when you do this to reduce the size of the mess.

Once you have cleaned out the drawer, turn the toaster upside down over the sink or dustbin and give it a light tap or shake to get any further crumbs out. If you want, you can use your cleaning toothbrush to carefully loosen some remaining crumbs in your toaster.

Once that is done, spray some of your all-purpose cleaner onto your microfiber cloth, and give the appliance a wipe on the outside. Don't spray directly onto your appliance, as this might cause it to break.

Kettle

The constant use of a kettle can result in hard water buildup inside your kettle. This is super quick and easy to get rid of. Simply fill your kettle with white vinegar and let it boil. Once it is done, dump all the vinegar out. You will most likely see that all the buildup will have disappeared. If not, repeat this process again.

Once you are happy with the result, rinse your kettle out thoroughly, and boil some water for a fresh cup of tea.

Fridge

Cleaning out the fridge can be a very time-consuming job. However, if you practice good maintenance in your fridge, you don't have to do a deep clean often. Proper fridge maintenance includes throwing out empty jars constantly and cleaning up spills as soon as they happen.

Unfortunately, deep cleaning your fridge is necessary from time to time. To do this, you will have to unpack all the contents of your fridge. Remove all the racks and baskets from your fridge. Spray the inside of your fridge with an all-purpose cleaner and let it dwell.

Wash all your racks and baskets in warm soapy water and dry them well. Now, wipe the inside of your fridge out, replace the racks, and then the food contents.

Pantry

Cleaning out your pantry is a job that is very similar to cleaning your fridge. If you maintain it by constantly throwing away empty jars and cleaning up potential spills, you don't need to do a deep clean often.

When you do want to deep clean it, you will need to unpack all the food that is in your pantry. Then, either spray your preferred all-purpose cleaner straight onto the racks in your pantry or spray it onto your microfiber cloth and then wipe the racks clean. If there are harder spills to clean, for example, olive oil, you can make a paste using baking soda and dish soap and scrub the spills with that. Remember to clean the baking soda paste off again using a clean, damp cloth.

Stovetop

Spills on stovetops should be cleaned after each mess. Otherwise, you run the risk of the spill caking onto your stovetop, making it very difficult to clean. When you practice general maintenance on your stovetop, remove all the knobs on your control panel first. A lot of grease and dirt gets trapped behind them.

Make a paste of baking soda and dish soap and use your cleaning toothbrush to scrub in all the little cracks. Once the dirt has lifted, clean the soap off with your microfiber cloth. You can use the same paste and methods to clean your actual stovetop.

Glass stovetops can be tricky to clean, particularly if the dirt has had time to settle and get hard on your surface. To clean these, sprinkle baking soda onto your stovetop. Next, cut a lemon in half. Use half of this lemon to squash out fresh juice all over your stovetop. The reaction of the lemon juice and baking soda will help the grease buildup lift more quickly.

Now, take the remaining half of the lemon to use as a sponge to rub all over your stovetop, and release more juice as you go. When lemon pips get squashed out, remove them immediately so they don't scratch your stovetop. Once you have scrubbed your entire stovetop with the lemon half, leave the lemon and baking soda to dwell on your stovetop for at least 15 minutes, then clean off.

Oven

Cleaning your oven is one of those jobs that everyone will have to do, but no one wants to do. This can be a difficult task, as old food spills in there can have gotten so stuck to your oven that it seems like they have become a part of the actual appliance.

The steps you will take to clean a self-cleaning oven will be vastly different from cleaning a non-self-cleaning one. Let's first look at how you should care for a self-cleaning oven.

The first thing you should be careful of if you ever want to clean your self-cleaning oven is not to disturb or scratch the pyrolytic coating in it. If you use the right tools in your oven, such as a soft sponge or cloth with a little bit of soap, this coating will stay in place.

Before you start cleaning your oven, make sure your space is well-ventilated. Turn on the overhead fan, open your windows, and move any pets you have far away from the kitchen. The smoke coming from your self-cleaning oven through its cleaning cycle can quickly fill up your space.

Next, remove everything from your oven. This includes oven racks and anything you might have in a warming drawer. Make sure you remove as many old food spills as possible. You can use a non-scratch scraper to do this by hand.

When this is done, you can set the oven on its self-cleaning function and wait for it to heat up and turn anything still left inside to a white dust. Once it is done and the oven has cooled off, you can take a damp cloth and wipe the inside of your oven out.

Now, let's look at how to clean a non-self-cleaning oven. As much as this is not most people's favorite job, it is something that should be done regularly, or at least every time you see spills in your oven. If you don't clean these spills up as soon as possible, they will become black and even harder to clean, and can cause your oven to smoke when you use it, affecting the flavors of the foods you are trying to bake.

Before you start cleaning your oven, you might want to layer newspaper on the floor to catch all the dirt that might spill. Remove the oven racks. You will clean those separately. Next, use a scraper to remove as many old food spills as possible.

Decide what products you want to use. There are many chemical oven cleaners on the market, but unless your messes in there are severe, you probably only need some dish soap, baking soda, a scourer sponge or pad, and some elbow grease. When you use products in your oven, be careful not to get them into the heating elements, coils, or fans if you have a convection oven.

Make a paste using dish soap, baking soda, and some water and apply it to your oven. Leave it to sit for at least 15 minutes before taking a damp scourer sponge or pad to scrub any remaining food spills off. When you are done, take a damp microfiber cloth to clean up the baking soda residue left in your oven. If you want, you can follow that up with another microfiber cloth and some vinegar to give it another rinse. That will help to break down any other pieces of grease or residue still left behind.

To clean your oven racks, give them a bath. You can put an old towel in the bath to prevent any scratches, and then put your oven racks on top of them. You can then either use a combination of baking soda and dish soap to clean them, or use dishwasher soap. If you use pods in your dishwasher, you can put them in your bath and then pour boiling water over them to dissolve the plastic coating. Then, fill your bath with water.

Leave your oven racks in the bath for a couple of hours to soak off any dirt on them. Take a non-scratching scourer sponge to gently scrub off any dirt or old food remains still left on your oven rack.

Range Hood

The range hood sits right above your cooking area and absorbs a lot of the smoke, steam, and grease resulting from cooking. It is important to clean this, not only to improve its ability to filter the smoke and grease, but also to avoid any odors in your kitchen. Luckily, this is not something you will have to do every week, but never leave it for more than six months between cleans.

To clean these filters, you will need hot water and a degreaser such as a dish soap, an enzyme cleaner, or OxiClean. Remove the filter from the overhead range hood and put it to bathe in boiling hot water with your degreaser of choice. Leave the filter in there for about 30 minutes. When you take it out and still see some speckles of grease on it, you can use a hard-bristle brush to clean it. Allow it to dry completely before you place it back in your range hood.

While your filter is soaking or drying, you can clean the rest of your range hood using a soapy sponge. Rinse it off afterward by using a damp cloth and wait until it is completely dry before you put the filter back in.

Garbage and Recycling Bins

There is nothing that can stink up a kitchen quite like a full garbage bin. To make sure your bins don't become a breeding ground for bacteria, make sure to clean them regularly.

First, remove the garbage bag. If your bag becomes smelly or if you have thrown out a lot of food scraps, don't wait until the bag is full before you take it out. Bacteria don't need a lot of time to grow.

Then, spray your bin thoroughly on the inside and outside with your all-purpose cleaner. You can also sprinkle some baking soda on the inside. If you can, do this outside. After you allow your product to dwell in your bin, then take a soapy sponge and give it a good clean. When you are done, rinse it off and dry it well with a microfiber cloth.

Chapter Summary

To make sure you have the right tools and cleaning products to clean your kitchen, here is a checklist of what you need to clean your kitchen.

In Your Caddy:

- microfiber cloths
- scourer sponge
- hard-bristle cleaning toothbrush
- rubber gloves
- non-scratch sponge
- a dish wand
- non-scratch scraper
- garbage bag
- all-purpose cleaner in a spray bottle
- antibacterial and/or disinfectant cleaner
- hydrogen peroxide (for cleaning cutting boards)
- lemon (for cleaning the microwave and stovetop)
- baking soda
- enzyme cleaner

Extra Equipment:

- vacuum cleaner
- broom and mop (if you have hard floors)
- Basket/box for cyclone cleaning

Chapter 7

The Bathroom

The bathroom is another room that can be overwhelming to clean. It must be done constantly, as this is a room where bacteria and other germs can sit if you don't keep your hand on it. It is a room that is used very frequently, and if there isn't proper ventilation, can easily be a breeding ground for mold and mildew.

If you have any natural stone in your bathroom, be careful of what cleaning products you decide to use. Should you decide to make your own cleaning products, remove the vinegar from the recipe, as this can cause discoloration on your stones. You can replace the vinegar in your recipe with plain water.

The Fast, Simple, Efficient System

The bathroom has enough space to clean to keep you busy for a whole week. However, if you follow the quick and easy cleaning steps in this chapter, you can clean everything from the toilet, basin, bathtub, shower, tiles, faucets, and mirrors in less than 30 minutes.

- Start out by doing your usual cyclone clean. Throw all empty bottles in your vanity or shower away, pack things standing around your basin in the vanity or where they belong, and remove anything that doesn't belong. This is a good time to also swap out the used towels in your bathroom for fresh ones.
- Dust all surfaces in your bathroom using your dry microfiber cloth. Remember to look at the windowsill as well, as dust can easily collect there when you open the window for ventilation before and after a bath or shower.
- Take your cleaner of choice—homemade, all-purpose, or bathroom cleaner—and spray your entire bathroom with it. While you let the product dwell, look at your tiles for any build-up of mold, mildew, or soap scum. If you see any, spray that as well. Apply toilet bowl cleaner to the inside of your toilet.
- Once your product has had time to sit, use a microfiber cloth to wipe all your surfaces. If you see any build-up in hard-to-reach corners around your faucets, use your bathroom cleaning toothbrush to clean it. Don't forget to clean your glass shower door (if you have one), as they can easily become unsightly due to soap scum buildup.
- When cleaning the outside of your toilet, you might want to use paper towels instead of a cloth to avoid any cross-contamination of bacteria that might sit around the porcelain throne.

- Once you have wiped all your surfaces, take your toilet brush and clean the inside of your toilet.
- Lastly, sweep, vacuum, and wash the floors in your bathroom.

Take a step back and admire your sparklingly clean bathroom, cleaned in under 30 minutes.

Let's Do Some Deep Cleaning

As much as doing a fast and efficient clean can help to maintain a generally clean bathroom, the buildup of bacteria, mold, mildew, and soap scum will require a deeper cleaning from time to time. Resist the impulsive urge to rather go shopping or watch a sports game. Even though it is a deeper clean, it still doesn't have to take you hours.

Toilet

We have explained the importance of doing the jobs you dislike the most first. For that reason, let's get into cleaning the toilet first. This is arguably the most unliked and intimidating job in the entire bathroom. If you take it step-by-step you can easily tame this fearsome beast.

Start with the toilet bowl closed, and spray the entire toilet with a general bathroom cleaner. After you have sprayed the top of the toilet lid, open it to also spray the seat and inside of the toilet. Then lift the seat, and spray the bottom of the seat and the rim. Remember to also spray the pipes at the back of the toilet, as that can be the perfect hiding spot for bacteria.

Next, take a toilet bowl cleaner and make sure to get the product right under the rim of the toilet. While you let that sit, take an enzyme cleaner and spray it on the floor around the toilet. This will help to break down any urine droplets or odors that may be present (which is most likely the case if you have young sons).

Once you have sprayed the entire toilet with your cleaner, use a cloth or paper towel to wipe and clean the entire toilet. If there are specific areas with extra buildup, particularly in small cracks or spaces, you can use a bathroom-only cleaning toothbrush.

After you have cleaned the entire toilet, take out your toilet brush and clean the inside of the toilet bowl. Think of it as brushing your teeth and clean the entire toilet on the inside thoroughly. When you are done brushing the toilet on the inside, close the toilet seat on the toilet brush so that the brush part is hanging on the inside. This way the droplets from the brush will fall directly into the toilet. After leaving the brush hanging like that for a while to dry, you can place it back in the toilet brush holder.

Remember that, every now and again, you will need to clean your toilet brush. If it is just a general clean, you can hold it over the toilet and spray it with a disinfectant and let it sit for at least 30 minutes. When you feel your brush is ready, rinse it under hot water and allow it to dry completely. Remember to also clean the toilet brush holder with disinfectant.

While on the subject of tools to keep your toilet clean, you should make sure you clean your plunger after every use. Spray it with your disinfectant of choice, leave it for at least ten minutes to dwell, and rinse it under hot water. Leave it to dry completely before you pack it away.

Glass Shower Doors

Soap scum can be extremely unsightly on glass shower doors, but can be easy to clean. All you actually need to do this is vinegar, a sponge, and water.

Apply your vinegar to your glass shower doors or screens and scrub the glass using a non-scratch sponge. The vinegar will help to lift the soap scum from the glass. Once you are done, rinse it well with water and dry your glass using a microfiber cloth.

You can also make your own glass door cleaner by mixing dish soap, vinegar, and water to clean your doors—you will find the recipe for this in my exclusive resource file. If you are too short to reach the very top of your glass, you can either use a stool, stepladder, or even a mop to be able to clean right at the top.

If your soap scum just doesn't want to budge, you can put some baking soda on your sponge, reapply your cleaner, and scrub the scum off. Remember to rinse the baking soda afterwards.

Once you have gotten rid of all the soap scum on your shower doors, there are many preventative steps you can follow to try to keep your glass shower doors as free from soap scum as possible. One of these is to dry your glass shower doors using a squeegee after every use. Do the same on the floors to avoid the buildup of mold and mildew.

Alternatively, you can also spray your glass shower doors with diluted vinegar after every use to reduce the buildup of soap scum.

If you have a shower curtain, you might notice that your curtain might also have a plastic liner on it. If either of these is either plastic, vinyl, or material, you can place them straight into the washing machine on a cold wash with some towels for a clean. Make sure you take the shower curtain rings off before you wash them.

When your curtain is done in the machine, you can hang it straight back on the shower rail to dry in the tub or shower.

Shower Tracks

If you have sliding shower doors, you will need to clean these tracks as well. These tracks can also become the ideal hangout for mold, mildew, and bacteria if they aren't cleaned regularly.

To clean it, throw some undiluted vinegar in the track and let it sit for a while. Then, use your bathroom cleaning toothbrush (not the same one you used in the toilet) to scrub the dirt and buildup clean. If you need to, you can also throw some baking soda in the track to scrub the dirt loose. Once you are satisfied, rinse it and dry the track well.

To prevent buildup from accumulating in these tracks, make sure to dry them after every shower. You can cover your finger in a microfiber cloth and run it along the track to dry.

Showerhead

Apart from the tiles in your shower, the shower door, and the door tracks, the showerhead will also need to be cleaned. A sign that this is needed is usually when your showerhead stops spraying the water in a clear line as it is supposed to due to hard water buildup inside it.

Since you shouldn't (and most often can't) open your showerhead up to clean it on the inside, you can do another trick. Take a plastic bag, fill it with undiluted vinegar, put it around your showerhead so it is completely submerged in the liquid, and tie it closed with an elastic band. Leave it overnight.

When you take it off the next morning, your showerhead should be good to go and you will probably be amazed at the water pressure your clean showerhead will provide.

Bathtub

For cleaning your bathtub, you can make your own cleaner— recipe to follow in my resource file. Spray this on your entire bath. Use a soft non-scratch sponge to clean the bathtub. If you have tougher stains or dirt marks on your bathtub, you can make a paste using dish soap and baking soda. Apply this using a very wet sponge and let it sit.

If your tub is white, you will not necessarily see the soap scum on it, so you can test by rubbing with your hand over the bath. If it feels smooth, it will be clean. If it feels rough, give it another wipe with your sponge.

Once you are happy with your tub, you can give it a good rinse and then either leave it to dry or take an absorbing cloth to dry it.

Basin

Basins in bathrooms are often filled with buildup from toothpaste and soap scum. To make sure you get rid of this, spray your basin first with a mixture of dish soap and vinegar, and then sprinkle some baking soda in it.

Leave this to sit for a couple of minutes, then use either a sponge or your bathroom cleaning toothbrush (not one you will use on your toilet) to scrub in the hard-to-reach places. Once you have scrubbed the basin, use a damp microfiber cloth to go over the entire basin, before rinsing and drying it (if you want).

Faucets

There are not a lot of things about a bathroom that can be as off-putting as visibly dirty faucets. Fortunately, these can be maintained in tip-top condition with a super quick cleaning routine.

Use your general bathroom cleaner, a mixture of dish soap and baking soda, or vinegar to clean your faucets. First, spray them and let the product sit for a couple of minutes. If there is dirt buildup anywhere on the faucet, use your bathroom toothbrush to scrub it. When you are done, you can rinse it and polish the faucets using a microfiber cloth.

Mirrors and Vanity

Cleaning mirrors in your bathroom can be another headache waiting to happen. You might think you are doing a brilliant job cleaning it just to cause unsightly streaks on it. However, it can be surprisingly easy to clean. Simply spray vinegar on your mirrors and then clean (top to bottom) with a microfiber cloth. This cloth shouldn't leave any streaks on your mirrors.

For the vanity cabinet, you can use an all-purpose cleaner. Spray it on the cupboard and then wipe dry with your microfiber cloth. Remember to also clean the door handles, as bacteria often sit on them.

Toothbrush Holder

While you are cleaning your vanity, pay special attention to your toothbrush holder. This is another trap that bacteria love. If you use a type of cup for a toothbrush holder, these get wet, slimy, and smelly on the inside if they are not cleaned out regularly.

If the cup you are using is dishwasher safe, you can simply put it on the top rack of your dishwasher to clean it. If you use a cup that is not dishwasher safe, you can pour some hot or boiling water with some vinegar into your cup at least once a week and let it soak. Alternatively, if you want to throw your toothbrush holder out completely, you can place your toothbrush on a washcloth and replace this cloth every couple of days.

Tiles

If you don't clean the tiles, and particularly the grout in between your tiles, regularly, buildup of fungi and mold can easily accumulate on them. The best product to use for cleaning your tiles and grout is a paste made using normal household products such as dish soap, baking soda, hydrogen peroxide, and tea tree oil. This recipe, together with the recipes for many other DIY cleaners, will be available to you in my resource pack. I will give more details on that later.

Apply your DIY tile cleaner to your tiles and grout using the soft side of a scourer sponge. Leave it to sit for a couple of minutes, then take the scourer side of the sponge to really work the product in. Once you are done, wipe the product off using a cloth.

When it comes to deep cleaning your bathroom floors, it can be easiest to just get down on your hands and knees and wash them by hand using a microfiber cloth. This type of cloth is great for picking up hair lying on the floor. Since bathrooms are generally small spaces, you might struggle to get into all the corners of your bathroom using a mop.

Spray your choice of all-purpose cleaner on the floors, let it sit for a couple of minutes, and then wash the floors in a zigzag pattern, starting from the furthest corner and working your way back to the door.

Chapter Summary

To make sure you have the right tools and cleaning products to clean your bathroom, here is a checklist of what you need to clean your bathroom.

In Your Caddy:

- garbage bag
- microfiber cloths
- rubber gloves if you prefer to use them
- paper towels
- toilet brush
- toothbrush for cleaning around the toilet (label this one or choose a different colored toothbrush))
- another toothbrush for general cleaning
- general bathroom cleaning toothbrush
- non-scratch sponge
- scourer sponge
- general bathroom cleaner in a spray bottle
- all-purpose cleaner
- toilet bowl cleaner
- tile cleaner
- vinegar
- basket for cyclone cleaning

Extra Equipment:

- vacuum cleaner
- broom and mop (if you have hard floors)
- Basket/box for cyclone cleaning

Chapter 8

Your Bedrooms

The bedroom is often a very neglected area when it comes to cleaning. In general, only you and your family will ever go into the rooms, so there is never that pressure to get it guest-ready before you have visitors over.

Since everyone has their own comfort level when it comes to dirt around the home, your bedroom likely shows this the most out of any room in your home. When you do clean your room, chances are you are only doing a quick clean.

Who has the energy to move a bed around in any way to clean behind and underneath it? Unfortunately, if you do allow dust to lay dormant in your room, you are setting yourself up for a whole host of possible allergies and other problems.

The bedroom has many different aspects that need cleaning. The most obvious might be the bed, nightside tables, and floor around it, but you should never forget (or neglect) to clean your mattress.

The Fast, Simple, Efficient System

Since many people don't spend a lot of time in their rooms—apart from sleeping and dressing—doing a **Fast, Simple, Efficient** clean in this room can really be quick.

- When it comes to fast cleaning your room, you can let your eyes do most of the work for you. Take your cyclone cleaning basket and garbage bag and remove everything that doesn't belong there. Put dirty clothes in the laundry hamper, take any dishes to the kitchen, put all your garbage in the bag, and the rest in your basket.
- Remove the bed sheets from the beds in each bedroom. Take them to the laundry and do a load of washing with all the bed sheets. In this way, the washing will get done while you clean the bedrooms. Make your bed with fresh linen. Having a neatly made bed will already make your room look a lot neater and cleaner.
- Use your dry microfiber cloth and dust your room. Look around the room at any spots of dust you see, and give them a quick wipe.
- Once you have finished dry dusting your room, spray your all-purpose cleaner of choice on all your horizontal surfaces or anything else that you see will need a clean. Pay attention to places you touch frequently, such as light fixtures or the handles of your closet.
- After you have allowed your product to dwell for a couple of minutes, wipe them off with a clean microfiber cloth.

- Finish the room by cleaning the floors. Whether you have hardwood floors or carpets in your room, start at the deepest corner of your room and work your way back to the entrance to avoid walking unnecessarily over your clean floors.

Six quick steps later and your bedroom will be clean enough to go another week. Repeat the process in any other bedrooms you need to clean.

Let's Do Some Deep Cleaning

As with any other room in your home, deep cleaning your bedroom from time to time will be inevitable. Don't be discouraged by the thought of cleaning your heavy mattress or moving your bed to clean the "storage container" that the area under your bed has become. There are ways to make even these deep cleaning tasks fast and simple.

Linen

Let's start out by discussing the first thing you likely see when you walk into your room: the linen on your bed. This includes everything from your sheets, duvet, other blankets, and pillows. It might also include a headboard.

When you clean your bedroom, it is good to start by cleaning your headboard. If you have a hard surface headboard, use a dry microfiber cloth to dust it. Should you have a material or upholstered headboard, you can vacuum it.

Your sheets and pillowcases should be changed and washed once a week. The sheets absorb your sweat, body oils, and dead skin every night, and if you don't clean them often, they can start to smell. Dirty pillowcases can also cause acne if they are not cleaned often enough. These you can simply take off and put in the washing machine.

Your Mattress

Using a mattress protector can help to keep your mattress as clean as possible. Otherwise, your sweat, body oils, and dead skin can seep into your mattress. Once this starts to smell, it can be quite the mission to get the odors in your room back to how you want it.

Once you have removed your mattress protector, or if you don't use one, you can clean your mattress by vacuuming it using an upholstery attachment. If your mattress has a funky smell, you can sprinkle some baking soda on it and let it sit for a couple of minutes before you vacuum it up.

It is good to leave your mattress open (with no linen on) with open windows in your room for the mattress to air out. This will also help to reduce any odors trapped in your mattress.

Under Your Bed

The space under the bed is often forgotten when it comes to cleaning. Many times, it is also used as storage where anything that you don't want to deal with or things that don't have a specific place in your home get placed.

Since a lot of dust and dead skin cells accumulate under the bed, it is important to clean there. This doesn't have to be done during every clean, but at least once every couple of months.

Remove everything that is under the bed and give it a proper vacuum. Use a dry microfiber cloth to dust everything before you place them back in your "storage container" under the bed.

Nightside Tables

Nightside tables next to the bed are often magnets for clutter. Even though they are supposed to only hold things you will need while you are in bed, they tend to get filled with junk and clutter that actually have other "homes" in your house.

Concentrate on these areas when you are doing your cyclone clean. Remove anything standing around that doesn't belong. Don't get lost in trying to declutter and sort through the stuff. That is a job for later.

Once you are done with your five-minute cyclone clean, take a dry microfiber cloth to dust these tables. Spray the all-purpose cleaner of your choice on your tables and wipe it off with a microfiber cloth. Remember to also dust nightlights, books, alarm clocks, or anything else you keep on your nightside table before you place them back in position.

Other Horizontal Surfaces

You might have other horizontal surfaces in your room. These can include a chest of drawers or dressing tables. As with your nightside tables, these other horizontal surfaces can fill up quickly with things that don't belong on them. Even if you have just deep cleaned your room, it won't look clean if the surfaces are cluttered.

Once you have removed everything from your surfaces, dust it off with a dry cloth, use your all-purpose spray, and clean your surfaces. Place everything you want to keep on these surfaces back in a clean and neat way.

Your Closet

Cleaning out your closet can be a massive job. Many people believe in cleaning out their closets seasonally to make sure the appropriate type of clothing is easily accessible. Whenever you decide to organize and declutter your closet is up to your personal needs.

Whenever you do organize your closet is a good time to also do a deep clean. Remove all the clothing from your closet. Then vacuum all the surfaces. You will likely be shocked to see the amount of dust that accumulates in a closet.

After you have cleaned out the dust, spray your choice of all-purpose cleaner on all your racks and wipe them with a damp microfiber cloth. Wait for the racks to dry completely before you pack your clothes back in.

If you have drawers in your room, remember to clean them out in the same way.

Children's Rooms

If you do have children, their rooms will obviously need a clean as well. Follow the same steps as you would cleaning your own linen, mattress, horizontal surfaces, closets, and floors. These rooms do come with an extra challenge: toys.

To instill good cleaning habits in your child (and since they were the ones making the mess), get them involved in packing away their toys. You can easily turn this into a game. The speed race works well with children of all ages. You can also incorporate other cleaning games to make the whole process fun and keep the tiny humans engaged in the process:

- **Cleaning Jenga:** Buy a standard set of Jenga blocks and write a cleaning chore on each block. When you and your children are ready to start, stack your blocks so that you can't see what chore is written on each block. Let them pull out a block and complete the task on it before they can take out another block.
- **Cleaning dice:** Write down the chores that need to be done and list them from one to six. Make sure there are equally good and bad chores on the list. Let your child roll a dice to determine which chore they should do first. Make sure they complete this task before they can roll again for another chore. Continue until they have completed all their chores.

Chapter Summary

To make sure you have the right tools and cleaning products to clean your bedrooms, here is a checklist of what you need to clean your bedrooms.

In Your Caddy:

- garbage bag
- microfiber cloths
- all-purpose cleaner in a spray bottle

Extra Equipment:

- vacuum cleaner
- broom and mop (if you have hard floors)
- Basket/box for cyclone cleaning

Chapter 9
The Home Office

The home office is another room in the house that is often hidden from guests and can, as a result, easily turn into a mess. During the COVID-19 pandemic, more and more people started working from home, resulting in living areas such as dining rooms doubling up as home offices.

This can result in your spaces being filled with cables, computers, and an endless amount of paper and stationery. If your home office is part of your living areas, you can include it in your zone dealing with the rest of the living areas. Alternatively, you can slot your home office into another zone, or even make it a zone on its own. Decide what works best for you and your space.

The Fast, Simple, Efficient System

If you keep your pile of documents and stationery neat, doing a quick clean of a home office doesn't have to take you more than just a couple of minutes to complete:

- Start with your cyclone clean. All your dirty coffee and tea mugs must go to the kitchen. Your jacket that has been hanging over your chair for a week can go to the laundry hamper. Take a separate basket for all your loose papers. You can sort through them later.
- Dry dust your space. This includes the computer, keyboards, table, chairs, and whatever else you might have in this space.
- Spray your all-purpose cleaner on your horizontal surfaces. Make sure you don't spray close to a computer or other electrical appliances. If the space is too tight to spray directly onto the surface, you can spray it onto your microfiber cloth.
- Wipe your surfaces to make sure they are clean.
- Do your final sweep of the room by cleaning the floors.

No matter how45 tempting it might be, don't just put that pile of papers you have removed back on the table. When you have a free minute after your day's cleaning, sort through them, file the important ones, and chuck the rest in the bin, recycling bin, or paper shredder.

Let's Do Some Deep Cleaning

Keeping your home office neat is a good start to having a clean space to work from. Since you might be spending a lot of time there, make sure to not delay doing a deep clean for months at a time.

Telephone and Cell Phone

You are most definitely using a cell phone every day and might even still have an old-school telephone in your home office. The touch screen on a cell phone and the buttons and receiver on a telephone can get extremely dirty without you even realizing it.

To clean it safely, you can use a mixture of rubbing alcohol and water, or any other mild and safe disinfectant. Spray some onto your microfiber cloth, and clean your cell phone or office phone with it. Never spray directly onto either of these types of phones. You don't want the cleaning product to seep into the actual phone.

Bookshelves

Bookshelves can easily become a dumping ground for books, papers, ornaments, and other junk that don't belong there. While doing your cyclone clean, remove as many of these things as possible.

Once you know what you need to keep on there, unpack all of the books. Use a dry microfiber cloth and dust the entire shelf. Move the shelf to clean behind it as well. Once you have removed the dust, spray it with your all-purpose cleaner of choice, and wipe it off after the product had time to dwell. Pack all the books that belong on the shelf, back.

Computers and Screens

The back of a computer screen, outside of a computer box, and the exterior of a laptop can be cleaned using a mixture of distilled water and some dish soap. Make sure the microfiber cloth you are using is only slightly damp, as you don't want to risk liquid running into any part of your computer. Gently rub the closed areas of your screen, computer box, or laptop, and dry it off with another microfiber cloth immediately.

The only product you should ever use to clean your computer or laptop screen is plain distilled water. Only use this if there is a mark on it that you cannot get off by using a lint-free microfiber cloth. Lightly dampen your cloth, wipe gently over your screen, and dry it immediately using either a dry part of the cloth or another lint-free cloth.

Computer Keyboards

Whether you are using a laptop or a computer with a separate keyboard, you don't want to use any liquid cleaning products to deep clean them. However, these keyboards can become extremely filthy with dead skin cells, dust, and crumbs, if you ever eat close to your computer.

A safe way to clean this is using a compressed air canister. Hold your keyboard vertically up at a slight angle so that the keys are facing down. Now spray with your air canister in between the keys and watch the crumbs and dirt blow out.

If you don't have a compressed air canister, you can also use a post-it note to clean your keyboard. Fold it into quarters and use the sharp points to slide in between the keys, loosening any dirt that may be trapped there. Alternatively, you can use your vacuum with a soft brush attachment. You can also buy keyboard protectors, which sit on top of the keyboard and keep the keys clean.

Once you have removed most of the crumbs and dust, you can spray your disinfectant of choice onto a microfiber cloth and wipe gently over the keyboard. Make sure the cloth is only slightly damp when you do this to avoid any excess liquid dripping into your keyboard.

You can follow the same tips to clean your computer mouse if needed.

Printer and Other Appliances

All office appliances, such as printers, paper shredders, and laminators, will need to be cleaned from time to time. A good indication that it's time to clean is when you see a buildup of dust or dirt on them.

Use a dry microfiber cloth to do your dusting. Then, put some distilled water mixed with dish soap on a cloth (make sure it is not dripping wet), and wipe your appliance on the outside. Then, use another cloth to dry it.

If your printer has a scanning facility, clean this scanner the same way you would clean your computer screen. First, try to just wipe it with a lint-free microfiber cloth. If there are any marks that don't come off from a dry wipe, use a tiny bit of distilled water or even some rubbing alcohol on a cloth, wipe it clean, and dry immediately.

Stationery

Leaving stationery lying around on your desk can immediately give the impression of an untidy office space. Even if you have a dedicated stationery holder, pens tend to lay all over the place. Making sure your stationery is sorted and packed in its place is more of a decluttering job, but is also important when cleaning.

When you do your cyclone clean, put all the stationery on your desk away. If you do want to keep some pens and highlighters on the desk, make sure they are neatly stacked in a stationery holder. Try to keep to having one pen at a time. There is no need to have six pens on your desk if you only really need one.

The more you keep your stationery packed away with only the absolute essentials on your desk, the quicker you will be able to clean your office space.

Papers, Documents, and Files

Unless you have gone completely digital, having loose papers lying around is inevitable in most home offices. Create a proper filing system whereby you only keep the documents that you really need, such as documents for tax purposes or for guarantees on appliances. Where you can, scan these documents to keep a digital copy on your computer rather than having it lay around.

Chapter Summary

To make sure you have the right tools and cleaning products to clean your home office, here is a checklist of what you need to clean your home office.

In Your Caddy:

- garbage bag
- microfiber cloths
- all-purpose cleaner in a spray bottle
- disinfectant or rubbing alcohol
- compressed air canister
- distilled water

Extra Equipment:

- vacuum cleaner
- broom and mop (if you have hard floors)
- Basket/box for cyclone cleaning

Chapter 10
The Laundry

If you don't stay on top of your laundry, it might feel like it is having babies every day. Every time you put on clean clothes, you create more laundry that, unless you buy new clothes daily, will have to be cleaned.

This will likely feel even worse after you cyclone clean the different zones in your house, as you are bound to find some piece of clothing lying around somewhere. Then there is the linen on your bed that will have to be washed regularly and the towels you use in the bathroom. This is not even to mention socks that go missing somewhere between the laundry basket, the washing machine, drying the clothes, and packing them away.

Washing your clothes in a machine is easy enough—you just put them in, add some detergent, and switch it on, right? But, there is drying. While using dryers is a common practice in many countries, particularly when you live in a colder climate, in hotter climates the norm is hanging your clothes to air dry.

While washing and drying your clothes can be done for you in a machine, there is no machine that will iron, fold, and pack your washing away for you. If you don't get to this immediately, you can easily create a mountain of clean clothes that belong in your closet. You might end up fishing clothes out of this mountain as you need them.

Having a pile of clean clothes somewhere in your house, no matter how well it might be hidden in a room, can really affect the overall neatness of your home as well as your own emotional and mental state. Conversely, staying on top of your laundry can be the boost you need to motivate you to keep the rest of your home also in a tip-top state.

To help you get through this never-ending task of staying on top of your laundry, you can create a weekly laundry schedule. You can do this by allocating different days for doing the specific items of laundry; for example, clothes on a Monday, towels on a Tuesday, bed linen on a Wednesday, and cleaning cloths on a Thursday. In my exclusive resource file, I have included a template of a laundry schedule that will make this task easy.

The Fast, Simple, Efficient System

Even though many people severely dislike doing laundry and it can seem like a massive job to do, it can be done quickly and efficiently in only a couple of easy (and surprisingly quick) steps:

- Read the labels on all your clothing items to make sure they are safe to machine wash, if they must be hand washed, or if you should take them for dry cleaning.

- Sort through your washing. Put all your whites in one pile, your darks in another, and your towels together. Also, look at the type of material you have. We will discuss the reasons for all of this below.
- Make sure you clean out all the pockets of your garment. Tissues left in a garment pocket can cause a massive mess that can take hours to clean. Pens left in pockets can cause ink stains. Turn delicate garments inside out.
- Load your washing machine, but don't overload it.
- Add the right amount of laundry detergent of your choice. If you use fabric softener, add it now. Alternatively, you can replace fabric softener with white vinegar and a few drops of essential oil.
- Select the cycle on your machine, and let it wash.
- When the machine is done, either put the laundry in the dryer or hang it outside to air dry.

Apart from doing the washing, your laundry room also needs to be cleaned. Follow the same process as you would in the rest of the house. Start with a cyclone clean and remove anything that doesn't belong in this room.

Dust can quickly collect in your laundry, especially if you use your dryer often. Dry dust the area. After that is done, spray everything that needs a wipe with your favorite all-purpose cleaner. Don't spray straight onto the buttons or settings knobs, as that may result in the cleaner getting to the wrong places and damaging your machine. Instead, spray your cleaner onto your microfiber cloth and wipe it clean. Finish it off by cleaning the floors in your laundry.

Let's Do Some Deep Cleaning

There will be times when your laundry will not be as simple as sorting your whites and darks, washing, and drying. There will be times when you will have to deal with removing stains, smelly towels, and whites that are looking more yellow than white.

When this happens, you will need to do the deep cleaning version of doing laundry. Luckily, there are surprisingly easy ways to deal with all these typical laundry issues.

Removing Stains

Unless you never eat or drink while dressed, your clothes are bound to get stains. The trick to removing stains is to tackle them as soon as possible. The quicker you work at treating your stains, the better your chances of getting rid of them altogether. If you catch it quick enough, you might be able to simply rinse them out under water or use a bit of laundry detergent.

However, if your clothes have stains that you know won't wash out, you can either look to buy one of the various stain removers available in your local supermarket, or make your own stain remover using hydrogen peroxide and dish soap. The complete recipe will be available in my exclusive resource file, available to you.

Draining Excess Water From Clothes

Sometimes your laundry can come out of the machine still dripping with water. Instead of putting it back in the machine for another cycle of spinning, you can use a simple towel trick.

Lay an absorbent towel out on a flat surface. Place your wet garment on top of it, and roll the towel (with the garment inside it) up to form a little snake. Take this towel snake on either side and give it a quick swing in the air. You can also tap it on your flat surface.

When you roll it out again, you will find that a lot of the moisture from your garment has now gone to the towel, leaving your garment a lot dryer. This hack is particularly useful when you have clothes that shouldn't go into the dryer and must be air-dried.

Removing Wrinkles

There is nothing as frustrating as taking your laundry out of either the washing machine or dryer and finding it full of wrinkles. That means you will likely not be able to simply pack your washing away, but spend possibly hours ironing the wrinkles out of your garments.

There are many ways to reduce and even remove any wrinkles from your laundry:

- Take your garments out of the washing machine as soon as it is done. If you leave them to sit wet in the machine, they will wrinkle.
- Hold the garments that you know tend to wrinkle by the bottom hemline and give them a good shake

before you either place them in the dryer or hang them to dry.

- If you see any visible wrinkles forming on your wet clothes, take your hand and smooth them out as much as possible.
- If you opt to hang them, put them straight onto a hanger and make sure they are hanging neatly.
- You can also put your already dry but wrinkled garments in the dryer with a damp cloth or towel. Put the dryer on for about 10 minutes. The dampness from the cloth will help to loosen the wrinkles in your garment.

The Weight of the Fabric

When sorting your laundry to wash, it can be helpful to consider the weight of the fabric. If you have a thick, heavy jacket, you will not want to wash it in the same load as your light cotton shirts. The same goes for towels that absorb a lot of moisture and can get quite heavy when wet.

If you do this, your machine will not wash your garments optimally, as it will not be able to distribute soap and water equally, and will not be able to drain the water properly. As a result, your garments can be dripping with water when you take them out of the machine.

Washing lightweight clothes with some heavy weights increases the risk of your lighter fabrics wrinkling in the wash, as they can be weighed down by, for example, your towels.

The heavier fabrics can also damage your lighter materials in the wash. This is due to the friction that is created between all the fabrics during the washing process. It can lead to your clothes looking worn out much quicker than they will if you are careful about what type of materials you wash together.

Delicates Bags

These bags are not just great for washing your delicate garments. You can also use them for washing socks. We all know that socks tend to go missing somewhere between the laundry hamper, the washing machine, and the dryer. You can avoid this by placing all your socks in a delicates bag instead of a laundry hamper, and washing and drying them in these bags.

If you have clothes made from material that can get damaged quickly by friction, you can wash them in a delicates bag as well. To protect these garments even more, turn them inside out when you wash them. This will result in any damage there might be to the garment, to be on the inside where only you will ever see it.

Pit Stains

If you wear deodorant or antiperspirant, you might have noticed yellow stains under the arms of your garments. This is commonly referred to as pit stains and is a result of body oils, sweat, and the deodorant or antiperspirant you use.

If this happens to your favorite white shirt, you don't have to throw the shirt away. You can make a paste of baking soda and water, put it on the stains overnight, and wash them as normal in the morning. This will reduce the appearance of any pit stains significantly.

Smelly Towels

Since towels are so super absorbent, they can quickly become smelly and stiff if they are not dried properly. You can reduce this by making sure you hang them in a well-ventilated bathroom, or if the weather allows it, outside to dry.

If your towels have reached the point where they become really smelly, you don't have to throw them out just yet. You can improve the appearance and smell of your towels by doing two cycles in your washing machine:

- First, load the problematic towels in your washing machine, and instead of laundry detergent, add a cup of vinegar to it.
- Once that is done, throw a cup of baking soda directly into the washing machine bowl and let it run for a second cycle.

These two products will work as a double whammy, cleaning your towels, softening them, and removing any odors attached to the material. Once your towels are clean, place them in the dryer or hang them outside to air dry. Make sure they are completely dry before you pack them back in the closet.

Whiten Whites

Seeing how your favorite white shirt is gradually becoming more yellow after every use and wash can be frustrating. However, you can save it and even return it to its former glory. Similar to treating pit stains, you can use a paste of baking soda and water as a detergent when washing your whites.

If you are still not happy with the results, you can soak your whites in hydrogen peroxide, vinegar, or boiled lemon juice. After you have soaked your whites, you can add any of these products straight to your machine as well for the wash.

After you have washed your whites and if the weather allows it, hang them in the sun to dry instead of just putting them in the dryer. The UV rays in the sun are great at lightening your whites.

Don't Overdo It

When it comes to loading your washing machine, make sure you don't overload it. You might be tempted to put an extra garment or two in to avoid having to do a second load. However, if you overload your machine, your laundry will not be able to move around properly inside the drum. This will result in your machine not cleaning effectively, and you might have to rewash the load again.

Always make sure you stay below the recommended limit for filling your drum. For optimal results, never fill your machine with more than three-quarters of the recommended load. This might mean that you will need to do another load, but your washing will come out clean.

Another place you must stick to the recommendation of your washing machine manufacturer is when adding detergent to your wash. You might be tempted to add a bit more detergent if you are washing really dirty laundry. However, more detergent will not result in a cleaner wash. Instead, it might result in detergent sticking to your clothes.

Stinky Shoes

Shoes such as trainers can easily be washed in the washing machine and either left outside to dry, or put in the dryer. Shoes in a dryer can make quite a noise as they are banging around. If this drives you up the walls, there are ways to work around it:

- Hang your shoelaces over the door of your dryer so that a piece of the laces is sticking out on the outside. This will prevent your shoes from playing the drums inside your dryer.
- Alternatively, you can put your shoes in a delicates bag and hang a piece of the bag over the door of the dryer.

If you find your shoes are getting stinky but their exteriors don't need a wash yet, you can put a couple of drops of your favorite essential oils on a cotton ball and place these balls in your shoes overnight. The bad odors will be replaced by the smell of your oils.

Your Washing Machine and Dryer

Make sure to maintain your washing machine by keeping it open after every wash until it is completely dry. If you keep it closed, it can create the perfect breeding ground for bacteria and can result in rust inside your machine. Clean the filter of your washing machine and the lint filter of your dryer regularly.

It is also important to clean the rest of your washing machine regularly. To clean the drum, you can pour vinegar either straight into the drum or in the detergent drawer and run the machine on its hottest cycle. You can also add a cup of baking soda to the washing machine and switch it on for a cycle. Clean the detergent drawers of your machine using a cleaning toothbrush and some vinegar.

If you see black mold forming on the rubber seal of your machine, you can use vinegar or a baking soda and dish soap solution to scrub it off. Make sure you don't damage the rubbers on the machine.

Chapter Summary

To make sure you have the right tools and cleaning products to clean your laundry, here is a checklist of what you need to clean your laundry.

In Your Caddy:

- garbage bag
- microfiber cloths
- all-purpose cleaner in a spray bottle
- laundry detergent
- hydrogen peroxide
- dish soap
- baking soda
- vinegar
- essential oil
- fresh lemon juice

Extra Equipment:

- vacuum cleaner
- broom and mop
- Basket/box for cyclone cleaning

Chapter 11

Other Areas of the Home

Sticking to your cleaning schedule and getting to all the zones in your home will improve the overall look and feel of your space. Your self-confidence will likely also get a boost, as you will quickly realize that even though you have struggled with getting your cleaning tasks done in the past, you are now acing it using the **Fast, Simple, Efficient** system.

Unfortunately, your house will likely have a couple more areas that don't fall under your cleaning zones. These are generally areas that either don't have to be cleaned weekly or they may be bigger jobs that will need more time to do. Some of these areas may include your garage, patio, hallway, and staircase. Since many people dread washing their windows, let's start by discussing how to complete this horrifying task.

Windows

The interior and exterior of your windows, your window frames, the casing of the windows, the tracks or windowsills, and window screens (if you have them) will have to be cleaned properly. The mesh screens on windows can usually clip off fairly easily, giving access to the window.

You can clean these screens either in the bathtub using a hand shower or jug with water, or clean them outside using a hosepipe. If your screens are very dirty, you can use any window or all-purpose cleaner and scrub the mesh gently using a soft-bristle brush.

To clean the interior of the window, spray either your choice of window cleaner or a mixture of water and vinegar onto the window, and use a flat-weaved microfiber cloth to clean the window, using the zigzag pattern. Many people prefer to use newspaper to wash their windows with, as it doesn't leave streaks. If you do this, try to find out what type of ink the local newspaper printers use, as some types of ink can cause damage over time. A flat-weaved microfiber cloth will also not cause any streaks, and with this, you don't have to worry about types of ink.

When it comes to the window frames and casing—the frame between the window frame and the walls—it is best to consider what type of material you are dealing with. If it is an older type of wood, for example, you might not want to use too much product on it, as it can damage older wood. If this is the case in your home, first try to clean it by using a dry microfiber cloth. Should you want to do a deeper clean, take a damp cloth to wash your old frames with. If you have modern frames and casing, you can use the cleaning product of your choice to clean them.

If you live in a colder climate where you experience a lot of condensation on your windows during the winter months, you should pay a bit more attention to your windowsills during these times. Condensation will drip down from your windows onto your windowsills. This can eventually lead to drips down the walls to your floors, or create a breeding ground for mold and mildew.

Take your cleaning toothbrush and remove as much mold and mildew as possible. Apply your cleaning product and let it dwell for about 10 minutes. Scrub the mold and mildew off using your toothbrush and dry the area using either a microfiber cloth or a paper towel. If you want, you can buy a mold and mildew protector from your local supermarket and treat the problematic areas of your home regularly.

Should you see any buildup of mold and mildew on your windowsills, it is best to treat them as soon as possible. You can use any product made specifically for mold and mildew, or you can create your own at home. Look out for this easy-to-make recipe in my exclusive resource pack!

When it comes to cleaning the exterior of your window, it is important to take note of the weather conditions on your cleaning day. The ideal condition to wash exterior windows is overcast days. If the sun is extremely hot on your window-washing day, it can bake the cleaning product onto your window if you are not quick and thorough enough in cleaning it off. Should you want to wash your windows in hot conditions, make sure you do this either early in the morning or late in the afternoon while the sun is not at its hottest. If you do go for an overcast day, make sure no rain is predicted.

Since the exterior of your windows can get very dirty, especially if they aren't washed regularly, a microfiber cloth might not be the best tool to use, as you will constantly have to rinse it out. Using a double-sided squeegee can make your life easier.

As with the interior, you can use any window cleaning product, or whip up your own product at home. Dip your squeegee in your product and make sure it is soaking wet. Go over the entire window with the wet part of your squeegee, and then flip it around to dry it quickly using the rubber side. If need be, you can use either a stepladder or a stool to reach to the very top of your windows.

To clean the exterior window frames and casings, you can use a dish wand with a nylon brush attachment. Fill it with your window cleaner, and release the product as you clean your windows.

If you want to clean exterior windows on second or third floors, you can follow the same steps as above, but attach your squeegee to an extendable pole. Otherwise, this might be a good time to rope in the professionals to clean your high exterior windows.

The tracks of sliding doors or windows can be another messy part of your home, and if you don't clean them thoroughly, the dirt in these tracks can eventually affect how your windows or doors open and close. Start this cleaning job by vacuuming as much dirt as possible. A brush attachment on your vacuum works well for this.

Once the dirt has been removed, use your dish wand with the brush attachment to wash the tracks. If you want, you can complete the task by drying the tracks using a microfiber cloth.

Linen Closet

A linen closet is a fantastic addition to any home, as you can keep all your sheets, towels, and often many other goods in there. Since this is the place you are storing your clean linen, you should try to schedule cleaning this closet out seasonally. That also gives you a great opportunity to throw out any towels that are damaged or completely worn.

To clean this cupboard, remove all your linen, vacuum or wipe your racks, and pack your linen neatly. A good trick to packing your sheets is to keep them together in sets. Take a pillowcase from a set, and place all the other linen belonging to that set inside that pillowcase. That way you will know you have a whole set when you want to change your bedding. This will save you a lot of time, as there will be no need to fish through all the linen in your closet and make everything untidy when you are looking for a complete set.

Staircases

If you have a staircase in your home, you probably prefer to skip this area altogether when cleaning. Unfortunately, there will come a time when you will have to get to this area.

Cleaning a staircase doesn't have to be as intimidating as it might seem. Since this is usually a clutter-free area, you might be able to skip the cyclone clean here. Always start at the top of the staircase and work your way down.

Take a dry microfiber cloth and dust the handrail and railing of the staircase. If your banister has small corners you will struggle to get into, use your cleaning toothbrush and a handheld vacuum. Follow this by spraying the all-purpose cleaner of your choice, and wipe it clean using another microfiber cloth.

The way you will clean the stairs themselves will depend on the material the stairs are made of. If you have hardwood stairs, you can either dry dust them using a microfiber cloth, a hand brush and a dustpan, or a dry microfiber spin mop. This mop can be super handy if your stairs protrude past the banister, as you can simply hold it over the railing to dust off those edges.

Once you have dusted the stairs, spray all-purpose spray on each stair, and wipe it with your microfiber cloth. Stairs are often easier to wash using just a cloth instead of a mop, as you don't have to worry about excess water spills from the mop. Take it step by step until you get to the bottom.

If your stairs are covered by carpet, you will need to vacuum them. Most staircases don't have power points to plug your vacuum in, so you will either have to use a battery handheld vacuum or use an extension cord.

An upright vacuum can be difficult to maneuver on shallow steps, so using a handheld or hose attachment vacuum will make the job easier. If you use a drum vacuum with a hose attachment, keep the drum of the vacuum either at the top or the bottom of the staircase. That way you avoid worrying about where to put the vacuum drum as you move. You might have to buy an extension hose if your hose isn't long enough, but it will be well worth the time and effort you will save.

Entryway

The entryway to your home is often filled with clutter, but also one of the most important rooms of your house. This is the first room guests will see as they walk into your house, and if this is not kept clean and neat, it can give the impression that the entire house will be in that state.

Unfortunately, this is also the area that can look like a landfill site if you are not careful. This is where you might place your bag or wallet, where your coat gets dumped, where your shoes get kicked off, and where keys and sometimes loose change gets tossed.

The good news is that since this area of the house is not lived in but merely walked through, you can keep it in a reasonable state by simply following the **Fast, Simple, Efficient** system of cleaning.

Take your basket and garbage bag and do a cyclone clean. Take the coats and shoes to the laundry or your room. Put any loose coins in your wallet or if you have a specific place you would like to keep them close to the door, pack them away. Place your keys where they belong. If there is mail lying around, put it in the home office. Sort through this mail as soon as you can after cleaning and throw away all junk mail or things you don't need to keep.

Dry dust all the flat surfaces in the entryway. Remember to also dust around the front door, as a lot of dust can accumulate on the doorframe. Spray your all-purpose cleaner on all your surfaces and wipe them clean using a microfiber cloth. If you have a front closet in your entryway, clean the doors and the handles, and also the doorknob of your front door. Finish it off by cleaning the floors.

If you do have a front or coat closet near your front door, remember to declutter this regularly. When doing this, clean the closet properly by dry dusting, vacuuming, and wiping the racks.

Hallway

Hallways are another area of a home that is often neglected when it comes to cleaning. However, from constantly walking up and down, a lot of dirt and dead skin cells can quickly settle on the floors. Luckily, hallways mostly consist of walls and floors, so they can be fairly quick and easy to clean.

If you have any horizontal surfaces such as a little table or shelf in your halfway, make sure they are free from clutter by doing a cyclone clean. Otherwise, you can go straight into dry dusting the space. If you have photos or paintings on the walls, make sure to dust them as well, as dirt often collects on the frames.

As you dust your hallway, pay attention to your walls. If you see any marks on them, clean these marks off quickly using baking soda and a damp sponge. Remember to wipe the baking soda deposits off the wall using a microfiber cloth.

If you have any horizontal surfaces or other areas of your hallway that will need more than dusting, spray the all-purpose cleaner of your choice and wipe with your microfiber cloth.

Once you have done dusting, it is time to get to the floors. If you have an area rug or runner in the hallway, start at the furthest point and vacuum it thoroughly. When you are done with the carpet, roll it up and put it out of the way. Now concentrate on cleaning the floors underneath the rug. Vacuum, sweep, and mop them, depending on the type of floors you have.

After you have cleaned the floors and, in the case of mopping, the floors have dried, you can roll your area rug or runner out again.

Garage

If you have a garage at home, you will likely agree that this space is far more than just a place to park your cars. Instead, it is often filled with tools, screws, paint, bicycles, gardening equipment, empty cardboard boxes, and often everything else you don't have a place for in the house. As a result, these spaces can get cluttered super quickly.

Apart from this, many garages in older homes don't have sufficient insulation and ceilings, resulting in a lot of dust accumulating there. This can be such a mission to clean that it seems easier to just close the garage door and forget about what is happening on the other side.

You can treat cleaning the garage the same way you would do any other room in your house, although, depending on the state of your garage, you will probably need to give yourself a bit more time to do so. Most garages need a good declutter once a year, as well as good storage solutions, so this is a job that needs more of a deep clean. You can still take a basket and garbage bag into your garage to clear the clutter, but you will probably need to dedicate a portion of your driveway for this.

Remove everything that is in the way, not in its place, or should be thrown out. If your garbage can fit in the bag, throw it away immediately. Alternatively, use a section of your driveway for stuff you need to throw away. If you plan this properly, you can arrange for a skip bin for when you want to clean your garage. If you have done so, throw everything that needs to go, straight into the bin.

Next, take your dry microfiber cloths and remove as much dust as you possibly can. If you have a vacuum with a hose attachment, you can use that to clear the dust, especially in higher hard-to-reach areas of your garage. Alternatively, you can put a microfiber cloth over a pole (or broomstick), attach it using a rubber band, and dust the corners of the ceiling with that.

Wipe off all your surfaces using an all-purpose cleaner and microfiber cloth. If there are greasy spots on any of your surfaces, you can get a degreaser at your local supermarket, or make your own product. Unless you have delicate surfaces in your garage, you can scrub them using a scourer sponge or a cleaning toothbrush.

Once all your surfaces are clean, it is time to get to the floors. Vacuum or sweep all the dust on the floors. Depending on what floor covering you have in your garage, clean the floors accordingly. If you have tiles or a cement floor, you can be generous with the amount of water you might need to clean the floors. If there are oil marks from a car being parked there, use a degreaser to clean it.

After you have washed the floors and either dried or allowed them to air dry, you can start to bring back everything that belongs in the garage. Try to sort your things so everything that belongs together is packed away in the same spot. Then, work through all the things that shouldn't go back into the garage. Throw away what needs to be dumped, and pack everything else where it actually belongs.

Porch and Patio

If you have outside living spaces at your house, such as a porch or a patio, you will have to schedule them also for cleaning. The frequency at which you clean these areas will vastly depend on the climate you live in. If you stay in a cold climate that gets a lot of snow, you will likely not spend a lot of time outside during the winter months. So, apart from clear snow on the way to the front door, you will likely not do a lot more outside.

However, if you live in a warmer climate where your winter days are still warm enough to enjoy the outdoors, your outdoor living spaces will need to be cleaned more regularly. These spaces shouldn't take you long to clean, depending on what furniture or potentially pot plants you have on them.

Start with a cyclone clean. If you have a pool close to your patio, you might have to deal with swimming towels lying around and possibly dishes. Remove everything that doesn't belong in that space.

Dry dust all the areas on your patio or porch where you can see dust. Let your eyes do the hardest work to tell you where to dust. You might notice cobwebs against your outside roofs.

You can clear this easily by sweeping the roof with a broom. Spray your all-purpose cleaner on all the areas that need cleaning, and follow that up with a wipe.

Most patios or porches have tiled flooring or decking. If your decking is waterproof, you can follow the same steps you would if you are cleaning tiled floors. Alternatively, clean your decking by sweeping them properly, and use cleaning product or water sparingly as needed to clean stubborn marks.

Your outdoor furniture will also need a clean from time to time. Depending on the material they are made from, you can dry dust them using a microfiber cloth or brush the dust off using a hand brush. You can follow this up with some all-purpose cleaner and a wipe-down. Many types of outdoor furniture are made from material that can withstand water, so if that is the case, you can also spray your furniture clean using a hosepipe.

If there are cushions on this furniture, look at the labels or tags for direction on how to clean them. If they are waterproof, you will likely be able to use the all-purpose cleaner of your choice on them and then spray them off with a hose pipe. If they are small enough to fit in your washing machine, you can clean them there. Alternatively, you can look at vacuuming the cushions and treating stains or marks on them with a stain remover.

Chapter Summary

To make sure you have the right tools and cleaning products to clean these other areas of your house, here is a checklist of what you need to clean these areas.

In Your Caddy:

- garbage bag
- microfiber cloths
- soft-bristle brush
- sponge
- vacuum
- cleaning toothbrush
- all-purpose cleaner in a spray bottle
- vinegar
- dish soap
- dish wand with a nylon brush attachment
- baking soda
- degreaser

Extra Equipment:

- vacuum cleaner
- broom and mop (if you have hard floors)
- Basket/box for cyclone cleaning
- double-sided squeegee
- stepladder or stool
- hand brush and dustpan
- microfiber mop or spin mop

Chapter 12

Keep It Clean

We have already discussed that cleaning is a never-ending job. Even after doing a thorough deep clean of your home, it will only stay clean for a couple of minutes. Enjoy your short victories every time!

Since there will always be new speckles of dust, another pair of dirty socks, and coffee mugs standing around, there will always be more things to clean. Changing your mindset from seeing cleaning as a practice rather than a project can help motivate you to keep cleaning.

Another thing that can help your new cleaning journey is creating good habits. This will include cleaning your tools after every use and doing a little bit every time. This can be as simple as putting that dirty coffee mug straight into the sink or dishwasher instead of just stacking it on the coffee table. A cleaning fairy won't magically take it to the kitchen. It will stand there until you do it.

The only times cleaning fairies will come is when you hire professional help. There are some jobs that are best left to the professionals. It is important to know when to do this and who to hire. Lastly, the more you work at decluttering your home, the easier it will be to clean and keep your home neat.

So, let's get into how you can keep your home clean, starting with your cleaning tools.

Clean Your Tools

There is no point in trying to clean using dirty cleaning equipment. Doing this, you will only create extra work for yourself, as you will spread the dirt on your cleaning tools, and will have to clean all the spaces again.

This is why it is important to always clean all your tools after every use. Then you know the next time you need to use a tool, that it will be clean. It is also much easier to clean fresh dirt off your tools than after allowing the dirt to dry on them. If you are unsure of how to best clean some of your tools, I have included a list of how to clean your tools fast and efficiently.

Brooms

To clean your broom, pick out as much debris or dirt as you can see between the bristles. Then, fill a bucket with warm water and add either a squirt of dish soap or oxygen bleach powder, and allow the broom to sit for about 30 minutes. After it has soaked in the soapy water, you can take it out and allow it to dry thoroughly before packing it away.

In general, you should be able to get a couple of cleans out of a broom before you need to clean it. Have a look at your bristles after every use and always try to remove the obvious dirt. This will reduce the frequency in which you would need to clean your broom.

Brushes

As you get into your cleaning routine and accumulate more tools, you will likely soon end up with at least a brush and a couple of cleaning toothbrushes. Cleaning these brushes will not only result in them cleaning better, but also lengthen their lifespan, as the bristles should stay in place for longer before they start to splay out to the sides.

To clean your brushes, remove as much of the debris in there as possible. You can do this straight over a dustbin and it should only take a minute or two to complete. Once this is done you can mix some oxygen-bleach powder with hot water and submerge your brushes in that for about 30 minutes. After they have soaked, you can dry them and pack them away.

Microfiber Cloths

Rinse your cloths out well in cold water before you wash them. This helps to get rid of any product left in your cloth after you have cleaned with it and also to remove any debris or dirt stuck to your cloth. You can also soak them overnight in warm water and detergent.

After you have rinsed and soaked them, you can put your cloths in the washing machine. It is best to wash your microfiber cloths separately, as they are designed to pick up debris and even other fabric types. Alternatively, you can put them in a delicates bag to protect your cloths. Never use any bleach or fabric softener when you wash them. Just use regular laundry detergent.

When you dry your microfiber cloths, don't use too much heat. It may be best to allow them to air dry.

Mops

Whether you have a flathead mop with a microfiber pad or a yacht or string mop with a removable head, you can rinse the pad or head well and then clean it in the washing machine. Alternatively, you can put the mop in hot water with some dish soap, let it soak, and then allow it to dry before you pack it away.

Rubber Gloves

Wearing rubber gloves while you are cleaning can be great at protecting your hands against hot water or harsh products. However, if you don't clean them well, you might be putting your hands into breeding grounds for many different types of bacteria.

To clean them, you can simply wash your hands while wearing the gloves using soap. Rinse them well. The most important part of cleaning your rubber gloves comes in removing them from your hands. Make sure you don't flip them inside out as you take them off, as this can result in moisture reaching the inside of your gloves.

Once you have taken them off, lay them flat over the edge of the sink to dry. Before you pack them away, you can sprinkle some baking soda in them. This will keep them dry and remove any odors that might build up inside the gloves.

Sponges

Give your sponges a good rinse, bending them in different directions while keeping them under running water. Make sure you get rid of any visible dirt or debris that might be trapped on the sponge. Once it looks clean, you can wring it out well to get as much water as possible out of it. Let your sponge stand up against the backsplash at your sink to dry completely.

Other ways you can clean your sponge include placing it in a bowl of water and putting it in the microwave for a couple of minutes, or throwing boiling water over it.

Unfortunately, no matter how well you clean your sponge, you will likely not be able to get all of the bacteria out of your sponge. This is why it is good to replace your sponge every couple of weeks, depending on how often you use it. Two easy signs that you should replace your sponge include discoloration or a nasty odor that you can't get rid of.

Squeegees

Over time and with regular use, soap scum can build up on the rubber tip of your squeegee. You can clean it by making a mixture of vinegar and dish soap. Apply it to your rubber tips using a sponge, scrub the soap scum off if necessary, and rinse well. Make sure it is completely dry before you pack it away.

The material part of the squeegee you can clean in the washing machine.

Toilet Brushes

We have briefly discussed cleaning your toilet bowl brush already, but sometimes this will need a deeper clean. When it is time to do this, fill a bucket with hot water and add some oxygen-bleach powder. Put the toilet bowl brush with its container into the bucket and allow it to soak for about 30 minutes.

After it has soaked, give it a good rinse and let it dry thoroughly before you pack it away.

Vacuum Cleaners

When it comes to cleaning your vacuum, it is important to first make sure your brush roller stays clean. This is the front part of the vacuum that rolls on your carpets and picks up all the dirt. If there are long strands of dirt or hair rolled around your roller, take a scissor and gently cut them loose.

Clean the filters of your vacuum cleaner regularly. Some vacuums have paper filters that need to be replaced. Others have washable filters. Remove the filter and either replace it, or rinse it off under running water. Make sure to check in your manufacturer's guide on how you should clean the filter of your vacuum cleaner.

The bin or canister in your vacuum should be emptied frequently, as an overfull bin can affect your vacuum's ability to suck. There are many different ways in which you can clean the bin in your vacuum cleaner—it is best to look in the instruction manual on how yours should be cleaned.

Keep Things Clean

Once you have established your routine of following your schedule to clean your house the **Fast, Simple, Efficient** way, do your best to create new habits to keep your space clean. In the beginning, it will take a conscious effort to create these habits. However, the more you do them, the more automated they will become.

The first thing you can concentrate on is doing your daily five every day. These are the non-negotiables that must get done that we discussed in Chapter 3. Some of the things on your daily five you might be able to do early in the morning, such as making your bed. Get into the habit of making your bed as soon as you get up in the mornings, ideally before you even leave the room.

The earlier in the day you can tick tasks off your list, the more accomplished you will start to feel in your new routine. Something simple like making your bed can help you to feel more organized and on top of things, which will, in turn, lead you to be more motivated to complete another small task.

Stick to your cleaning schedule as far as possible and try to clean your zone of the day as soon as you can. If you clean using the **Fast, Simple, Efficient** system, it will take you less than 30 minutes to complete an entire zone. Once you have cleaned your zone, you will be able to relax and enjoy a sense of accomplishment.

In the beginning, don't worry too much about "the deeper clean." Start with baby steps. Focus on your daily five and clean one zone a day. If you are having a bad day, just try and get your daily five done. If it's a really bad day, then just try and do one or two things on your Daily Five list or put it off and catch up later in the week. This is why I've suggested leaving a couple of days free when you create your schedule.

Accept that there will be times when specific events or the way you feel will keep you from sticking to your schedule and that's okay. When this happens, don't be too hard on yourself. Just try your best the next day to get back to your routine. The **Fast, Simple, Efficient Cleaning System** is designed to be flexible. Make it work for you and your situation. The schedules you create are not set in stone. If something isn't working then change it. I use this system in my home and I have changed my cleaning schedules several times.

Another good habit to create is to deal with things immediately. Don't simply put your stuff down to deal with "later." Who knows when that "later" might come? Clutter on spaces can be like real magnets. If you put one thing down, soon you will see three or four things standing out of place.

Instead of putting something down, get into the habit of putting them away immediately. Make sure everything in your house has a place. If you know exactly where to put something, you will waste less time and energy deciding where to put something. Putting something away when you know exactly where it must be shouldn't even take a minute of your time.

Call in the Professionals

Unless you are a professional cleaner—which is very unlikely if you are reading this book—it is important to know that there will be times you should get help. This is particularly the case for cleaning jobs that you will schedule into your annual calendar, such as washing off gutters or barge boards or deep cleaning your sofas or mattresses.

Another cleaning task that can be good to leave for professionals is cleaning the exterior windows of a second or third story, as we mentioned in the previous chapter. They will come with ladders or scaffolding to clean your windows safely using harnesses.

A general rule you can use in determining whether a job should be left to the pros or if you should attempt to do it yourself is to look at the equipment you will need. Unless you have an upholstery cleaner or extractor, there is no point in spending hundreds of dollars on buying one that you will only use once a year.

Another rule you can follow is deciding if you are capable of performing a specific task. If you are afraid of heights or clumsy, there is no need for you to climb on a ladder to clean the high exterior surfaces of your home. Should you fall while cleaning, your medical bills will be way more than what you would spend on getting a professional to do it. If you know that you will never be motivated to do a particular cleaning job, and you can afford it, then pay a professional to do it for you.

When it comes to hiring professionals to do your annual, difficult jobs, there are many factors you should consider. One of the most obvious ones is the costs involved. Some professionals' prices can seem like they will break the bank. Others may seem too good to be true. Decide how much you are willing to spend on the professional, and then see who is available for your price range. You don't want to spend hundreds of dollars on a job if you can get someone to do it for cheaper. Conversely, you also don't necessarily want to go for the cheapest cleaner if you are not sure their quality will be good enough.

This is why reviews on cleaners can be so helpful. These days most cleaning services will have some sort of an online presence, whether it is having their own website or a page on a social media site. Look at these pages for images of jobs they have completed, and most importantly, look at the reviews other clients have left.

You can also ask for advice from your family and friends. They might have used an upholstery cleaner recently. Ask them about their experience with the cleaner and their satisfaction with the job.

Lastly, remember that when you hire a professional cleaner, you will allow this stranger into your personal space. Make sure this cleaner is trusted (the reviews will help with this) and if you feel comfortable with them. Phone the cleaner or company to schedule your job instead of doing it online. If you like the vibe you get during the telephone conversation, you can book them. Trust your gut.

Declutter

Once you have cleaned your home and created healthy habits to keep it neat, you can look at decluttering your home. This step is all about getting rid of things you don't need and storing the things you do need to keep and use regularly, in a neater and more user-friendly way.

This might sound simple, but decluttering your home can be one of the most difficult tasks to do:

- You will create a mess doing this, as you will have to sort through all your belongings.
- Making the decision on whether to keep something or not is not easy. You will deal with a lot of "what if I will need it again" situations.
- You have spent a lifetime collecting your clutter, so getting rid of it can be emotionally exhausting.
- And while we are on the topic of emotions, you might even have family heirlooms that you will never use, but hold on to for sentimental reasons.

See, I told you decluttering can be difficult. This is why you should focus on the benefits it brings. You will spend less time searching for things. You will have less clutter to organize and pack away. Your quick cyclone cleans will become even faster. Most importantly, having less stuff filling up your physical space will result in having a clearer mind.

Luckily, there is no need to feel overwhelmed by the thought of decluttering your space. I will be there with you, helping you every step of the way. So, keep an eye out for the next book in this series, where we will discuss and tackle everything that has to do with decluttering.

Chapter Summary

The same way that cleaning your house revolves around little tasks you should do continuously, so is keeping your home clean. This might sound more complicated than it has to. In fact, you can do this by just following a couple of steps:

- Clean all your equipment after every use. There is no point in trying to clean a counter using a dirty cloth.
- Create good cleaning habits. Do your daily five tasks every day, as early as you possibly can. Never leave things for "later," as this "later" can take weeks to come. Deal with things immediately by packing them away instead of putting them down.
- Start with baby steps. Complete your daily five and clean one zone a day. The **Fast, Simple, Efficient System** is flexible so make it work for you.
- Know when you will need professional help. If you don't have the tools or capabilities and might hurt yourself trying to complete a cleaning job, you might want to call in the pros. Decide on what you are willing to spend on getting the job done and look at reviews to help you decide who to hire.
- Declutter your home regularly. A clear space will result in a clear mind— something we all need.

Now, complete your cleaning routine by admiring your neat home every time you come through the front door. Be proud of yourself.

Conclusion

You now have all the knowledge, tools, and processes you will need to make cleaning your home **Fast, Simple, and Efficient.** If you implement these in your home, you will not only change the way you clean, but also the cleanliness and overall neatness of your home. Let's look at some of the important steps and principles of **The Fast, Simple, Efficient Cleaning System**:

- Get it done. It doesn't have to be perfect.
- You don't have to deep clean every time you clean.
- Create your cleaning schedules.
- Complete your daily five cleaning tasks each day.
- Use the zone cleaning system.
- Use efficient cleaning techniques.
- Create cleaning caddies for different zones.

Conclusion

Using these principles, you will know that you can clean an entire area in your home in less than 30 minutes. All you need to do is just follow these three easy steps:

1. Start with a **cyclone clean**.
2. **Dust** and then **wipe** your surfaces.
3. Clean your **floors** and remove the **rubbish**.

Throughout the book, I have promised access to my exclusive resource file. This file is filled with tips, schedules, checklists and DIY recipes I use daily:

- daily five, laundry, and weekly zone cleaning schedules
- an example of a weekly zone cleaning schedule
- monthly, seasonal, bi-annual, and annual cleaning checklists
- a tracker for cleaning tasks ("When did I last...")
- more than 20 homemade cleaning recipes
- a list of pet-friendly essential oils

These checklists and schedules will help you to implement **The Fast, Simple, Efficient Cleaning System**. To get your copy of this file as well as many other tips and tricks to make your life and daily tasks easier, use the link or QR Code.

https://bit.ly/CleaningResourceFile

Now that you have the knowledge of how to clean your home **The Fast, Simple, Efficient** way, allocate your zones, create your schedules, take it step-by-step, and create the clean home you have always wanted. Remember, *just get it done; it doesn't have to be perfect.* You can do it!

If you have enjoyed the content of this book and think it can help others as well, please leave a review, let others know about this book, and help me change more people's lives.

Click on the link below, and it will take you to my book's sale page, or you can scan the QR code.

https://bit.ly/ADHDCleaningBuy

Scroll down the page, and on the lower left-hand side, click on "Write a customer review." Reviews are so important to us small authors, so I would really appreciate it.

About the Author

Lily Beacham was originally a high school teacher and worked with many students who had ADHD. One of her daughters also has ADHD, so she has always strived to help young people to succeed by putting systems in place to help them cope with the challenges they faced.

She also has a background in interior design and home organization. She has used her skills to create systems that help people with ADHD with tasks such as cleaning, decluttering, organization, and productivity. Her strategies have helped countless people, and now she wants to help you, too.

ADHD Solution Deck: Cleaning is the first book in a series that will arm you with the knowledge, tools, and processes that can make cleaning fast, simple and efficient and transform your life.

Lily lives in a beautiful beachside community with her husband and pets. She is surrounded by coastal walks, national parks, and pristine waterways, and she enjoys the laid-back lifestyle. She loves nothing better than being surrounded by her family and friends. Lily loves to cook, read, and learn new things, but most of all, she loves to help people.

Lily Beacham Books

Website: https://www.lilybeacham.com/

Facebook: www.facebook.com/ADHDLilyBeachamBooks

Facebook Group: https://bit.ly/
ADHD_Support_Lily_Beacham_Books

Instagram: www.instagram.com/adhdlilybeachambooks/

References

Abramson, A. (2022, January 20). *5 ways to tweak your cleaning routine if you have ADHD*. Apartment Therapy. https://www.apartmenttherapy.com/adhd-cleaning -routine-tips-36991822

ADDitue Editors. (2022, March 31). *Real-world strategies: "How I stop being so impulsive."* ADDitude. https://www.additudemagcom/how-do-I-stop-being-impulsive-adhd/

American Lung Association. (n.d.). *Cleaning supplies and household chemicals*. https://www.lung.org/clean-air/at-home/indoor-air-pollutants/cleaning-supplies-household-chem#:~:text=VOCs%20and%20other%20chemicals%20released

Brown, A., & Ask a house cleaner. (2020). How to clean stairs [Video]. *YouTube*. https://www.youtube.com/watch?v=25cLShA1h28

Hakim, H. (2021, June 9). *Cleaning with ADHD: Why is it so difficult? What can you do?* Hyper Lychee. https://www.hyperlychee.com/blogs/arti-cles/cleaning_with_ _adhd#:~:text=The%20best%20way%20to%20actually

Holly. (2022, August 29). *10 cleaning games to make chores more fun*. Simplify Create Inspire. https://www.simplifycreateinspire.com/cleaning-games/

Hutchinson, B. (2020, August 15). *Hyperfocus — at your service*. ADDitude. https://www.additudemag.com/hyperfocus-at-your-service/

Jaksa, P. (n.d.). *The disorganized adult*. ADHD Center. https://www.addcenters.-com/articles/the-disorganized-adult

Kolberg, J. (2022, July 13). *33 ADHD-friendly ways to get organized*. ADDitude. https://www.additudemag.com/how-to-get-organized-with-adhd/

Lisa. (2021, February 12). *Zone cleaning how to guide*. Money Minded Mom. https://www.moneymindedmom.com/zone-cleaning/#:~:text=Zone%20-cleaning%20is%20a%20simple

Maker, M., & Clean my space. (2011a). How to clean a flat screen TV [Video]. *YouTube*. https://www.youtube.com/watch?v=L6h5olaQEgQ

Maker, M., & Clean my space. (2011b). Clean your self-cleaning oven [Video]. *YouTube*. https://www.youtube.com/watch?v=spD_D6bJ-X4

Maker, M., & Clean my space. (2013). How to hand wash dishes [Video]. *YouTube*. https://www.youtube.com/watch?v=qddGMCplL2o

Maker, M., & Clean my space. (2014a). 5 nasty things in your bathroom [Video]. *YouTube*. https://www.youtube.com/watch?v=H47JQTwCcQA

References

Maker, M., & Clean my space. (2014b). 5 nasty things at the office [Video].
YouTube. https://www.youtube.com/watch?v=nvUZZQoYRVE

Maker, M., & Clean my space. (2014c). Wood furniture cleaning secrets [Video].
YouTube. https://www.youtube.com/watch?v=RKWm6EqlSSM

Maker, M., & Clean my space. (2014d). Clean greasy range hood filters [Video].
YouTube. https://www.youtube.com/watch?v=k2FltIbCaDk

Maker, M., & Clean my space. (2014e). 5 vacuuming tips that suck [Video].
YouTube. https://www.youtube.com/watch?v=nY6SPCxsc4U

Maker, M., & Clean my space. (2015). Tile scrub [Video]. *YouTube*. https://www.y-
outube.com/watch?v=RlGrcMEV6c8

Maker, M., & Clean my space. (2016a). How to clean a laptop [Video]. *YouTube*.
https://www.youtube.com/watch?v=iR3LlEU_HRU

Maker, M., & Clean my space. (2016b). Living room cleaning routine [Video].
YouTube. https://www.youtube.com/watch?v=WvCz_gZxjcw

Maker, M., & Clean my space. (2017). 7 expert cleaning tips you need to be
using [Video]. *YouTube*. https://www.youtube.com/watch?v=-C-ic2H24OU

Maker, M., & Clean my space. (2018). Pro cleaning tips [Video]. *YouTube*.
https://www.youtube.com/watch?v=6O-QpJrrji4

Maker, M., & Clean my space. (2019). How often should I clean it [Video]?
YouTube. https://www.youtube.com/watch?v=owLYcemHBrc

Maker, M., & Clean my space. (2020a). How to clean a shower and glass doors
[Video]. *YouTube*. https://www.youtube.com/watch?v=jKcGILf3hWs

Maker, M., & Clean my space. (2020b). How to clean everything in your
bathroom [Video]. *YouTube*. https://www.youtube.com/watch?v=cP3f6_9_oh8

Maker, M., & Clean my space. (2020c). How to clean everything in your kitchen
[Video]. *YouTube*. https://www.youtube.com/watch?v=wHBQNIkwWYQ

Maker, M., & Clean my space. (2020d). How to clean your cleaning tools
[Video]. *YouTube*. https://www.youtube.com/watch?v=z6uRdFubU_A

Maker, M., & Clean my space. (2020e). How to clean an oven (non self cleaning)
[Video]. *YouTube*. https://www.youtube.com/watch?v=RiI4i0lLs3E

Maker, M., & Clean my space. (2020f). How to clean everything in your bedroom
[Video]. *YouTube*. https://www.youtube.com/watch?v=JQKp10dR3Co

Maker, M., & Clean my space. (2021a). How to clean windows like a pro [Video].
YouTube. https://www.youtube.com/watch?v=6e5IMM1mrTc

Maker, M., & Clean my space. (2021b). How to clean floors (hardwood, laminate
and luxury vinyl) [Video]. *YouTube*. https://www.youtube.com/watch?
v=zwI8R7rUg EU

Maker, M., & Clean my space. (2021c). My top 10 dusting tips [Video]. *YouTube*.
https://www.youtube.com/watch?v=vd5OFpcNuN0&t=53s

Maker, M., & Clean my space. (2022a). 12 laundry hacks that will forever change your laundry game [Video]. *YouTube*. https://www.youtube/watch?v=pmgZvok8AyA

Maker, M., & Clean my space. (2022b). How to clean a bathtub [Video]. *YouTube*. https://www.youtube.com/watch?v=RlGrcMEV6c8

Maker, M., & Clean my space. (2022c). How to clean oven racks with very little effort [Video]. *YouTube*. https://www.youtube.com/watch?v=prsVpiGx0bI

Maker, M., & Clean my space. (2022d). 5 ways to make your house smell great [Video]. *YouTube*. https://www.youtube.com/watch?v=K0PDuDNFDhI

Maker, M., & Clean my space. (2022e). 10 cleaning hacks for people who hate to clean [Video]. *YouTube*. https://www.youtube.com/watch?v=wzpOeLft8KY

Reynolds, C., & Clean my space. (2019). Let's clean the garage out [Video]. *YouTube*. https://www.youtube.com/watch?v=aiBT1nBmf8w

Silva Casabianca, S., & Tartakovsky, M. (2021, March 1). *ADHD impulse control: 5 tips to help you manage*. Psych Central. https://psychcentral.com/adhd/adhd-in-adults-5-tips-for-taming-impulsivity

Silver, L. (2020, November 9). *Manage your distractions*. ADDitude. https://www.additudemag.com/manage-your-distractions/

The Cleaning Lady. (2020, November 5). *How to keep your house clean with ADHD*. Confessions of a Cleaning Lady. https://confessionsofacleaninglady.com/ house-cleaning-tips/adhd-cleaning/

.

Milton Keynes UK
Ingram Content Group UK Ltd.
UKHW020750151223
434437UK00019B/951